Copyright © 2019 Warner Bros. Entertainment Inc.
HARRY POTTER characters, names and related indicia are ™ & © Warner Bros. Entertainment Inc.
WB SHIELD: ™ & © WBEI.
WIZARDING WORLD trademark and logo © & ™ Warner Bros. Entertainment Inc. Publishing Rights © JKR (s19)

www.harrypotter.com

ISBN 978-1-338-32296-5

10 9 8 7 6 5 4 3 2   19 20 21 22 23

Printed in the U.S.A.   40 • First printing 2019 • Text by Maria S. Barbo

Illustrations by Patrick Spaziante • Origami design by Janessa Munt • Book design by Betsy Peterschmidt

Special thanks to Sam P. and Lesley Thelander

* The more lightning bolts, the more difficult!

INSIDE the MAGIC

ORIGAMI is the Japanese art of folding paper into **ANIMALS**, **OBJECTS**, **CASTLES**, and more! Each Hippogriff, phoenix, owl, and magical item you will learn to craft in this book can be broken down into a series of basic folds and shapes. It's helpful to practice the basic folds before combining them into more complicated pieces.

Here's an up close look at the basic folds and structures you will master over the course of this book.

TIP: We recommend completing these pieces in order of the book.

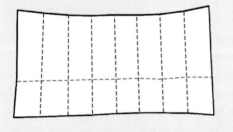

CREASES

Lines that you make by folding paper are creases. Creases are important in origami because they prepare the paper to fold in other ways later on. In fact, the earliest steps in each origami piece are all about making creases. Creases are indicated by dotted lines. Take a look at how creases will appear in this book below.

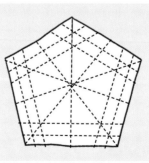

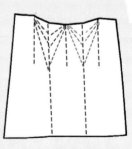

NEED HELP MAKING THE MAGIC HAPPEN?
Use a Popsicle stick or any other hard (but not sharp!) edge to help press down your folds into creases.

FOLDS

The two most basic folds in origami are the **VALLEY FOLD** and the **MOUNTAIN FOLD**.

VALLEY FOLD

A valley fold is made when you start with your paper color-side down and make a fold. See how the crease dips down into the paper? If you look at the paper from the side, it should look like a "V" or a valley. That's a valley fold!

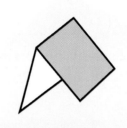

MOUNTAIN FOLD

To make a mountain fold, start with your paper color-side down and make a fold the opposite way. The fold should stick up like a ridge or a mountain.

PRACTICE MAKES PERFECT!

If you're just starting out, try warming up on your own large paper. Some of the pieces in this book are complicated and it will be easier to see the shapes and folds if they are bigger.

SQUASH FOLD

You will use a squash fold in almost every piece in this book. A squash fold is when you take a flap that's 3-D and flatten it to make it 2-D. Here are the basic steps:

1 A squash fold starts with a flap.

Flap

2 Stick your finger in the flap to open it up.

3 Do you see the crease running down the middle of the flap? Press down on it with your finger.

This fold becomes this crease.

4 Now **SQUASH IT**! Press down on the crease to flatten. The side creases you folded earlier will help.

Press here.

Helpful side creases   Helpful side creases

You just mastered the **SQUASH FOLD**!

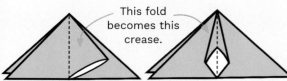
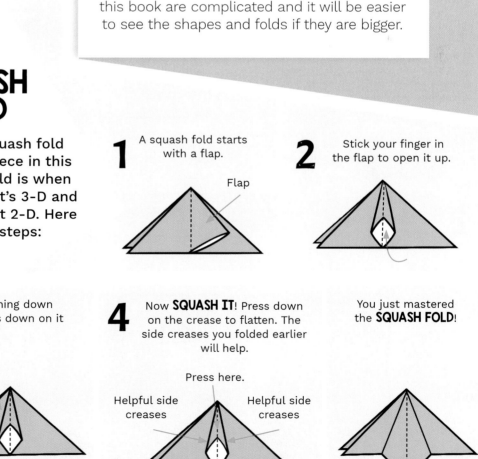

INSIDE REVERSE FOLD

When you make an inside reverse fold, you create a pocket or flap by tucking a fold of paper down and in between two other layers of paper. It's called a reverse fold because you turn a valley fold into a mountain fold—or a mountain fold into a valley fold.

Inside reverse folds are usually used to make the heads or tails of origami creatures.

To practice making an inside reverse fold, start with a piece of paper that's been folded diagonally into a triangle. The color side should face up.

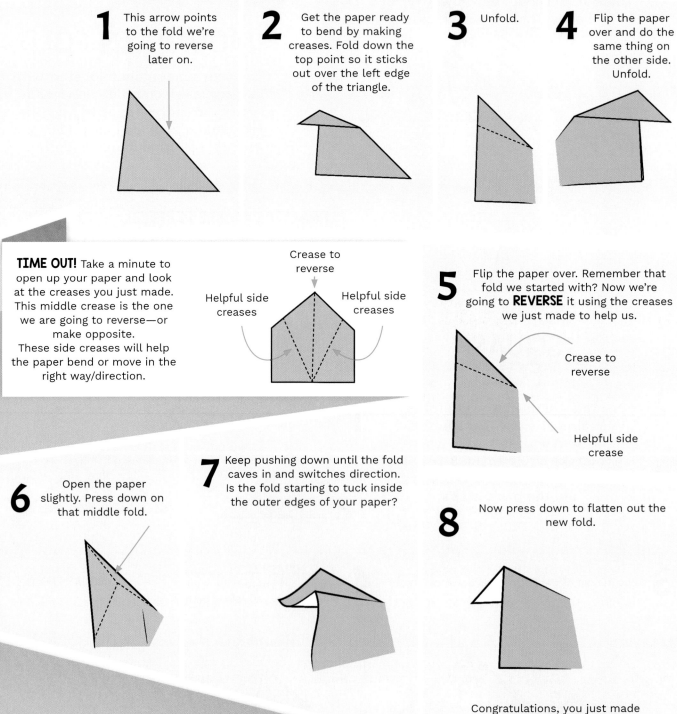

1 This arrow points to the fold we're going to reverse later on.

2 Get the paper ready to bend by making creases. Fold down the top point so it sticks out over the left edge of the triangle.

3 Unfold.

4 Flip the paper over and do the same thing on the other side. Unfold.

TIME OUT! Take a minute to open up your paper and look at the creases you just made. This middle crease is the one we are going to reverse—or make opposite.
These side creases will help the paper bend or move in the right way/direction.

Crease to reverse

Helpful side creases   Helpful side creases

5 Flip the paper over. Remember that fold we started with? Now we're going to **REVERSE** it using the creases we just made to help us.

Crease to reverse

Helpful side crease

6 Open the paper slightly. Press down on that middle fold.

7 Keep pushing down until the fold caves in and switches direction. Is the fold starting to tuck inside the outer edges of your paper?

8 Now press down to flatten out the new fold.

Congratulations, you just made an **INSIDE REVERSE FOLD**!

OUTSIDE REVERSE FOLD

These folds are similar to inside reverse folds, except the new flaps end up on the outside instead of tucked in between two layers of paper. Outside reverse folds are also used to shapes heads—like the head of the Hippogriff—and tails.

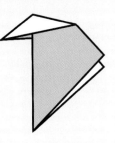

1 To practice, start with a piece of paper folded into a triangle. Fold the tip over to make a crease—just like you did for the inside reverse fold.

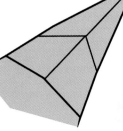

2 Open it up. Push the tip back along the side creases. Right now they are valley folds, but they are about to become mountain folds! Push the fold away from you.

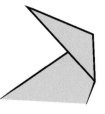

3 As you press, the top crease will reverse as well.

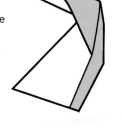

4 Press to flatten. You did it!

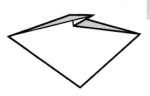

7

RABBIT EAR FOLD

Rabbit ear fold (sometimes just called "rabbit folds") are fun because they create long flaps that look like rabbit ears. They can be used to make owl wings or to hold the edges of a Chocolate Frog box together.

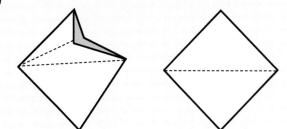

1 By the time you are ready to fold a rabbit ear, you will have already made several key creases. These creases will help the paper bend and fold the way you need it to.

2 Push in on the sides of the point at the same time. Your paper will bend into a flap that sticks straight up.

3 Press that flap to the side to flatten it. You've just added a **RABBIT EAR FOLD** to your origami skills!

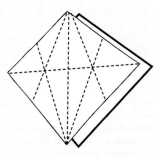

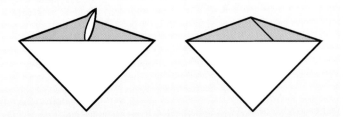

BASES

Now that you've practiced basic folds, it's time to move on to **BASES**. Most of the origami creatures and objects in this book start from the same three bases: a **KITE BASE**, a **SQUARE BASE**, or a **BIRD BASE**. Master these and you'll have a shortcut when you work on more complicated pieces later on!

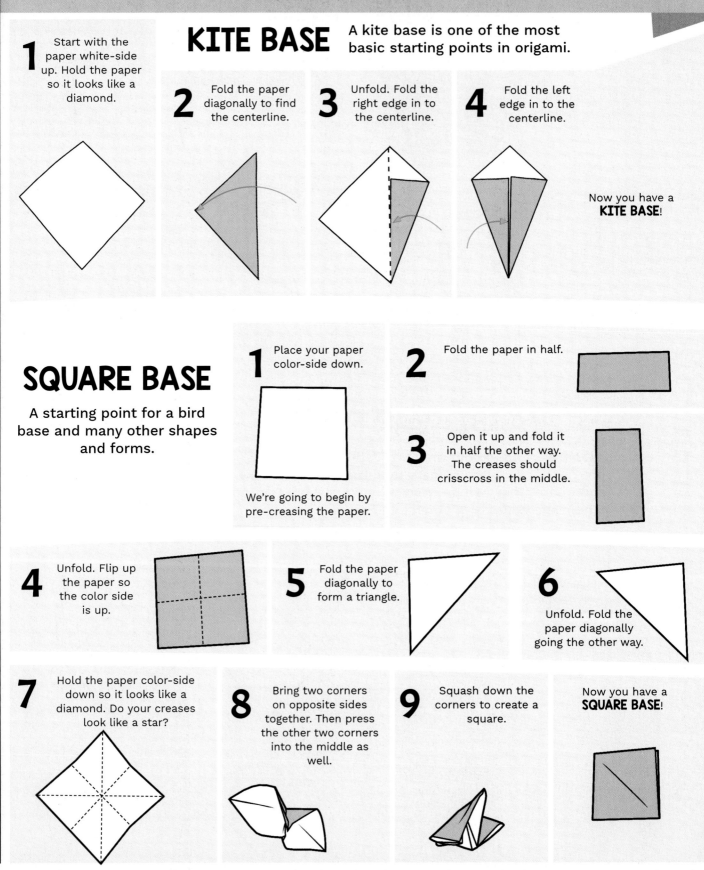

KITE BASE

A kite base is one of the most basic starting points in origami.

1 Start with the paper white-side up. Hold the paper so it looks like a diamond.

2 Fold the paper diagonally to find the centerline.

3 Unfold. Fold the right edge in to the centerline.

4 Fold the left edge in to the centerline.

Now you have a **KITE BASE**!

SQUARE BASE

A starting point for a bird base and many other shapes and forms.

1 Place your paper color-side down.

We're going to begin by pre-creasing the paper.

2 Fold the paper in half.

3 Open it up and fold it in half the other way. The creases should crisscross in the middle.

4 Unfold. Flip up the paper so the color side is up.

5 Fold the paper diagonally to form a triangle.

6 Unfold. Fold the paper diagonally going the other way.

7 Hold the paper color-side down so it looks like a diamond. Do your creases look like a star?

8 Bring two corners on opposite sides together. Then press the other two corners into the middle as well.

9 Squash down the corners to create a square.

Now you have a **SQUARE BASE**!

8

BIRD BASE
AND PETAL FOLD

1 To create a **BIRD BASE**, rotate your square base so it looks like a diamond.

Make sure the side that opens is facing down.

2 Fold the right edge to the centerline. Press down to crease.

3 Fold the left edge to the centerline. Press to crease.

4 Flip the piece over. Repeat steps 2 and 3 on the other side.

5 Fold both layers of the top triangle flap down. Press to make a crease.

6 Unfold all the flaps.

7 Lift up the top layer of paper.

8 Push it back against the horizontal valley fold.

9 The sides will start to come in like a petal. Press the bottom edges down and in first. The folds on the top edges need to be reversed so it may take a little more effort to get them to lie flat.

10 Congratulations! You just made a **PETAL FOLD**!

11 To move on to the bird base, flip your piece over.

12 Fold down the small triangle in the middle to make a horizontal crease. Then fold it back up.

13 Repeat steps 2-9 (but skip step 4) to make a petal fold on the other side.

14 Bring the point of the bottom flap up to meet the top point and press it flat. Now you should have two narrow triangular flaps on the bottom.

Congratulations, you now have a **BIRD BASE**!

Now that you've mastered the basics, you're ready to move on! With adult supervision, begin by cutting out the paper at the back of the book. As you build your pieces, reference the illustrations of each step to make sure you're folding the correct parts of the paper.

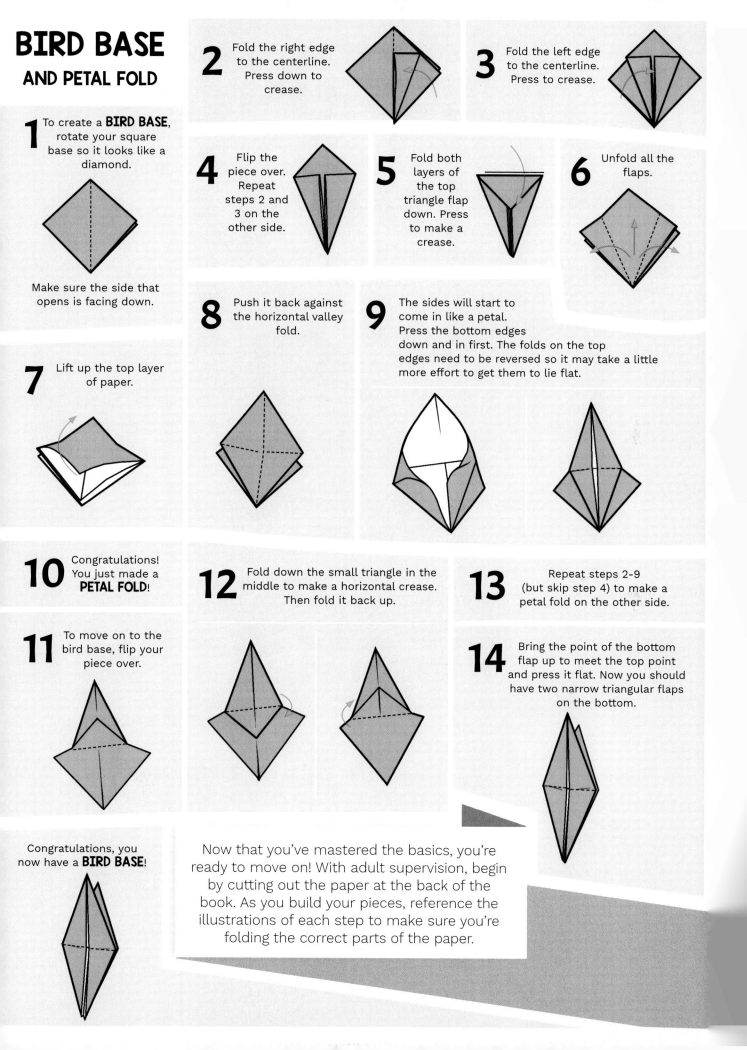

SORTING HAT

Students are sorted into Hogwarts houses via the **SORTING HAT**, an enchanted magical object. The Sorting Hat is able to read incoming Hogwarts students' minds and determine if they belong in Ravenclaw, Gryffindor, Hufflepuff, or Slytherin. Sometimes—such as in the case of Draco Malfoy—it is able to determine a student's house very quickly, and sometimes—like in the case of Harry Potter—it needs a bit more time to communicate with its wearer.

DIFFICULTY: ⚡⚡⚡⚡⚡

How to Make the SORTING HAT

Find out which Hogwarts house you belong in! Start with a kite base. You can find this information in the introduction page on page 8.

1 Unfold the kite base. Your creases should look like this:

2 With the color-side down, fold this tip down to meet point A.

A

3 Rotate the piece. Now fold the sides in to make two long triangles.

Press to crease.

4 Fold the base of the the hat up about 1/8 of an inch. Press to crease.

5 Fold the base of the hat under at these two points.

6 Rotate the piece. Fold edge A to line up along edge B. Press to crease.

B

A

7 Now, it's time to make the hat floppy! We will add three **PLEAT FOLDS**. Unfold step 6, but before unfolding all the way, make a crease slightly above the diagonal one as shown.

TIP: Think of the pleat fold as a 3-D wrinkle!

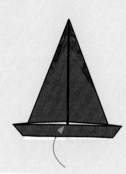

8 For the second pleat fold, fold point A to point B. Then repeat step 7.

B

A

9 Repeat step 7 again at the top to make the third and final pleat fold.

B

A

10 Curl the sides back to make the hat 3-D.

DONE!

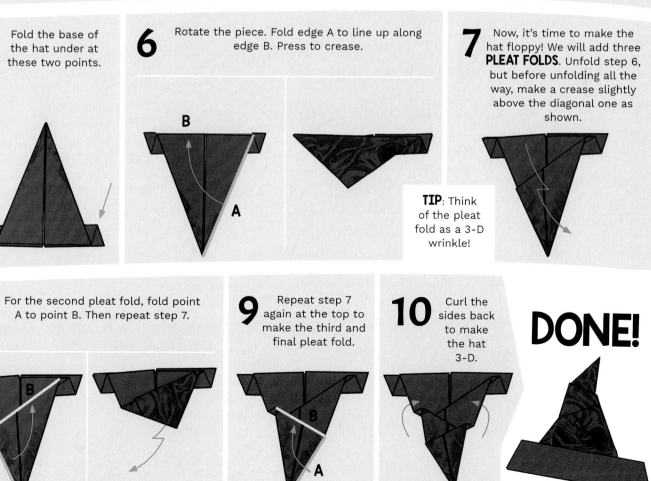

CAULDRON

At Hogwarts, **CAULDRONS** are predominantly used in Potions class—or in the girls' bathroom when Hermione is brewing in secret. Cauldrons are favored by witches and wizards because they can be used over a heated fire to create potions such as Felix Felicis and Polyjuice Potion. Cauldrons are also on the required school supplies list for incoming students at Hogwarts.

DIFFICULTY: ⚡ ⚡ ⚡ ⚡ ⚡

How to Make a CAULDRON

Brew some potions in your own cauldron! But maybe don't add any *real* potions— remember, this is still made out of paper.

1 Place your paper potion-side up. Before we make the cauldron, we'll need to prepare the paper by making lots of creases.

2 Fold your paper in half. Make sure your paper matches the image below. You may have to rotate it.

3 Unfold. Fold in the two outer edges to meet the centerline.

4 Unfold. Rotate your paper and fold it in half the other way.

5 Unfold. Now fold these outer edges in to meet the centerline.

6 Unfold. Notice that the creases you just made form a grid. These creases will help you create the shape of the cauldron later on.

7 Fold the paper diagonally to form a triangle.

8 Unfold. Fold the paper diagonally in the other direction.

9 Open up your paper. The pattern of creases on your paper should look like this:

13

10 Fold the bottom left corner A to meet point B. Press to crease. Unfold.

11 Repeat step 10 in all four corners. Unfold. Your paper should look like this:

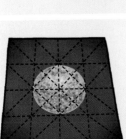

12 Now we're going to use all the creases you just made to make the cauldron 3-D.

This end will pop out.

Push.

Push.

Pinch in one corner to make a rabbit ear.

13 Repeat step 12 on all four corners. Flatten. It should look like a pinwheel.

14

On the corners without handles, bring edge A to edge B.

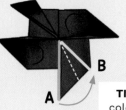

15

Fold edge A to edge B. Repeat on the other side.

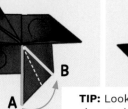

TIP: Look at the colors to help you.

16

Take this corner and fold it back and under the piece along the dashed white line.

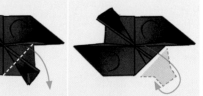

17

Repeat on the other side.

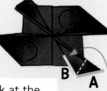

18

Use your fingers to pull from the middle to open up your box. The base should form a square with the feet at the bottom.

19

Fold down the sides that stick up by joining edge A to edge B.

TIP: Press into a crease on the inside.

20

Fold down any additional paper that is sticking up and press so that your opening is rounded.

21

Pull out the two feet on the bottom of the cauldron so it stands up.

DONE!

14

HOWLER

ONE PART
(with two pieces!)

A **HOWLER** is an enchanted letter that could probably just say its message quietly, but instead it, well . . . howls it, making the Howler an effective choice of punishment for unruly children, as well as an effective form of communication from the Improper Use of Magic office at the Ministry of Magic. Only when the Howler's message is complete (and after a lot of embarrassment) does it self-destruct.

DIFFICULTY:

How to Make a HOWLER

Who would you like to send this Howler to? What will you write on the inside? You will need scissors, a pen, and a stapler for this piece of origami. Make sure to have them at the ready—and always use scissors with adult supervision!

1 With adult supervision, cut off the white part of your paper and save it for later. It will be used starting in step 21.

2 Place the red paper color-side down.

3 Fold the paper in half lengthwise so the color side is now facing out.

4 Take the bottom corner and fold it over to the left edge to form a triangle.

5 Cut off and discard the triangle.

6 Fold the remaining rectangle in half the long way by bringing the right edge to meet the left.

7 Unfold. Fold it in half the other way by bringing the bottom edge to meet the top.

8 Unfold. Fold both edges to the center.

9 Unfold. Fold the bottom right-hand corner over to the left edge to form a triangle.

Crease here.

10 Unfold. Do the same on the left side.

Crease here.

11 Unfold. Now make the same creases on the top corners.

Crease here and here.

12 Unfold. Your new creases should look like this. All these creases will help you make the folds in the next steps.

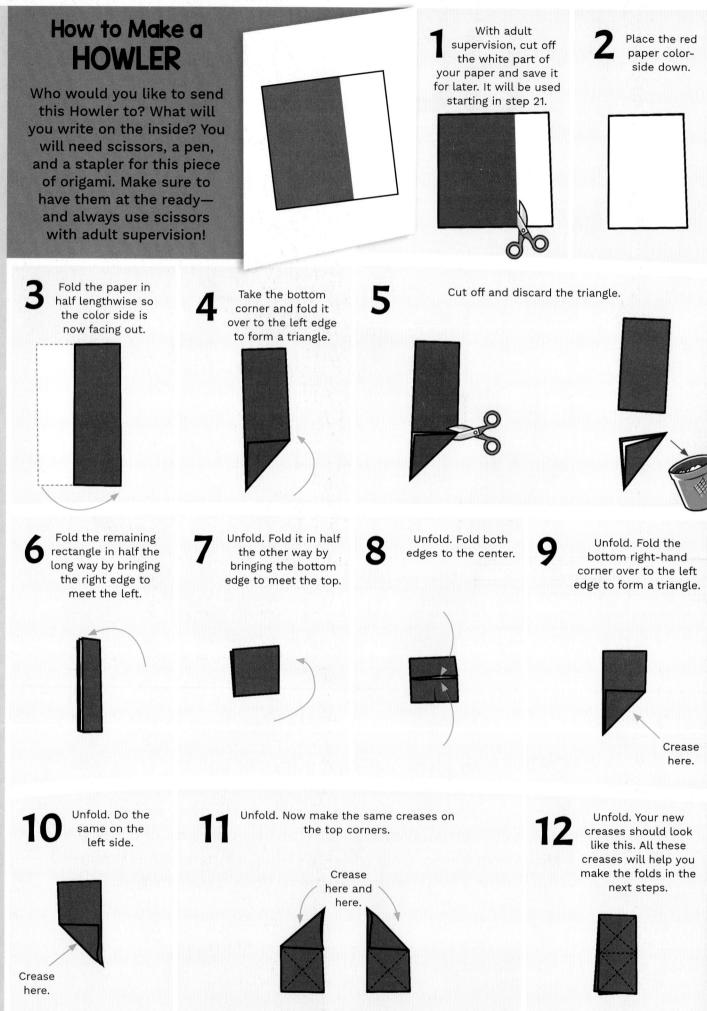

16

13 Dog-ear the bottom left corner.

14 Dog-ear the bottom right corner.

15 This will be the base of your envelope. Your piece should now look like this.

16 See the diamond in the middle of your piece?

Pinch all the creases of the diamond so they become mountain folds.

17 Form a smaller diamond by pinching mountain folds within the diamond you made in step 16.

Pinch here (both sides).

18 Unfold. Inside reverse fold the left-hand corner. Do you see your Howler starting to take shape?

19 Inside reverse fold the bottom right-hand corner.

The bottom should look like a triangle.

20 Curl the top corners back.

Set this piece aside.

21 Place the scrap piece in front of you.

22 Fold it in half.

23 Cut along the crease you just made.

24 Fold one piece in half lengthwise, but only crease the bottom edge.

Crease here.

25 Unfold. Fold the right edge to the small crease you just made. Press to crease the entire edge.

Cut mark.

Crease mark.

26 Cut along that crease. Discard the small strip.

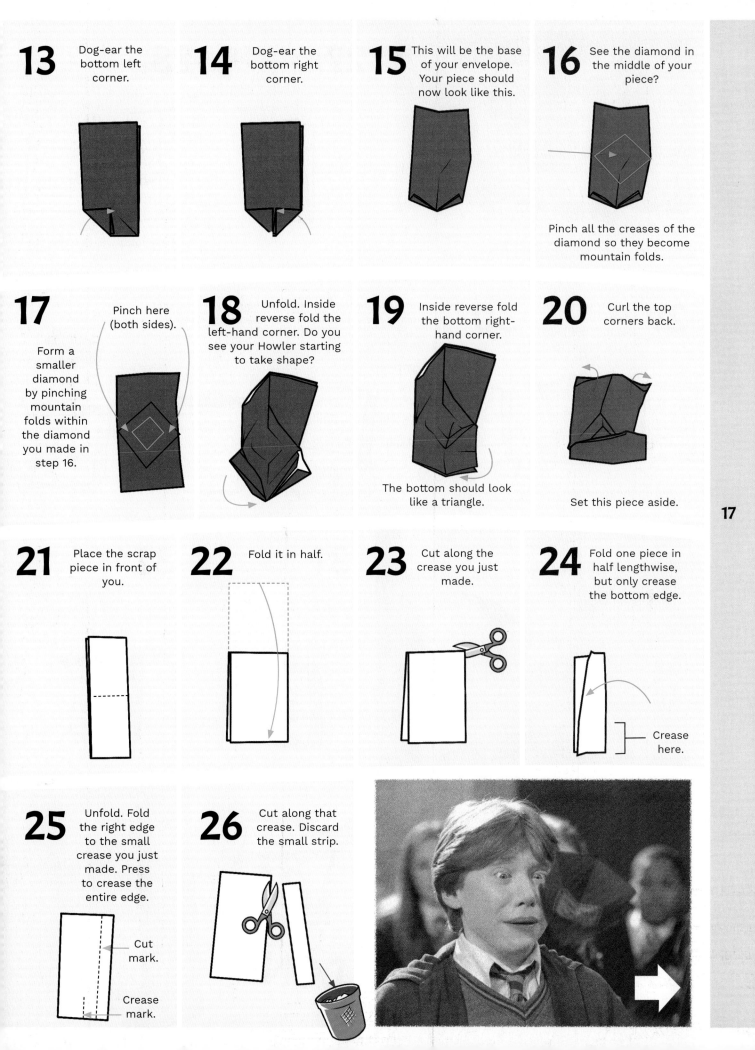

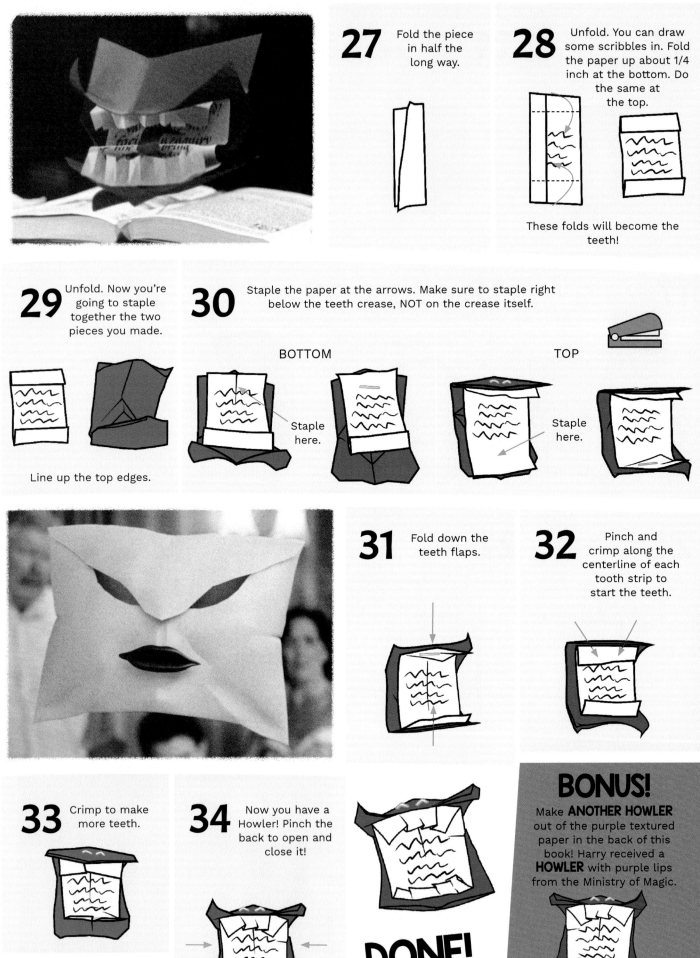

27 Fold the piece in half the long way.

28 Unfold. You can draw some scribbles in. Fold the paper up about 1/4 inch at the bottom. Do the same at the top.

These folds will become the teeth!

29 Unfold. Now you're going to staple together the two pieces you made.

Line up the top edges.

30 Staple the paper at the arrows. Make sure to staple right below the teeth crease, NOT on the crease itself.

BOTTOM

Staple here.

TOP

Staple here.

18

31 Fold down the teeth flaps.

32 Pinch and crimp along the centerline of each tooth strip to start the teeth.

33 Crimp to make more teeth.

TIP: Re-pinch the mountain folds from step 17 to ensure your Howler is ready to go.

34 Now you have a Howler! Pinch the back to open and close it!

DONE!

BONUS!
Make **ANOTHER HOWLER** out of the purple textured paper in the back of this book! Harry received a **HOWLER** with purple lips from the Ministry of Magic.

CAT

ONE PART

CATS are very special animals in the wizarding world. They are among the three permitted animal companions that a student may take to Hogwarts (the other two being a toad and an owl), and they are also a form that an Animagus may take. An Animagus is a person who can transform themselves into an animal. Professor McGonagall can transform herself into a tabby cat, and it is in this form that we first meet her in *Harry Potter and the Sorcerer's Stone*.

DIFFICULTY: ⚡ ⚡ ⚡ ⚡ ⚡

How to Make a
CAT

Here you'll be able to make a cat. Be it Animagus or a regular tabby, this paper creature can watch over you!

1 Start with the color-side of the paper facing down. Fold the paper in half.

2 Unfold. Flip the paper over and fold both edges into the center.

3 Fold this rectangle in half by bringing edge A to meet edge B.

B

A

4 Unfold.

5 Take the bottom left flap and fold it out to make a crease that starts at point A and ends at point B.

Do the same on the other side.

A

6 Unfold those flaps.

7 Fold the right flap back along the new crease you just made.

Do the same on the other side.

8 Unfold.

9 Fold the right corner in so it lines up along the nearest crease. Repeat on the other side.

10 Fold the flaps back along the first crease you made.

11 Fold the piece down in half again.

12 Fold it back up and make a pleat fold 1/4 inch down from the centerline.

Flip the piece over.

13 Fold down the top corners of the body shape as far as they will go without ripping or stretching the paper.

14 Unfold the corners and inside reverse fold them in.

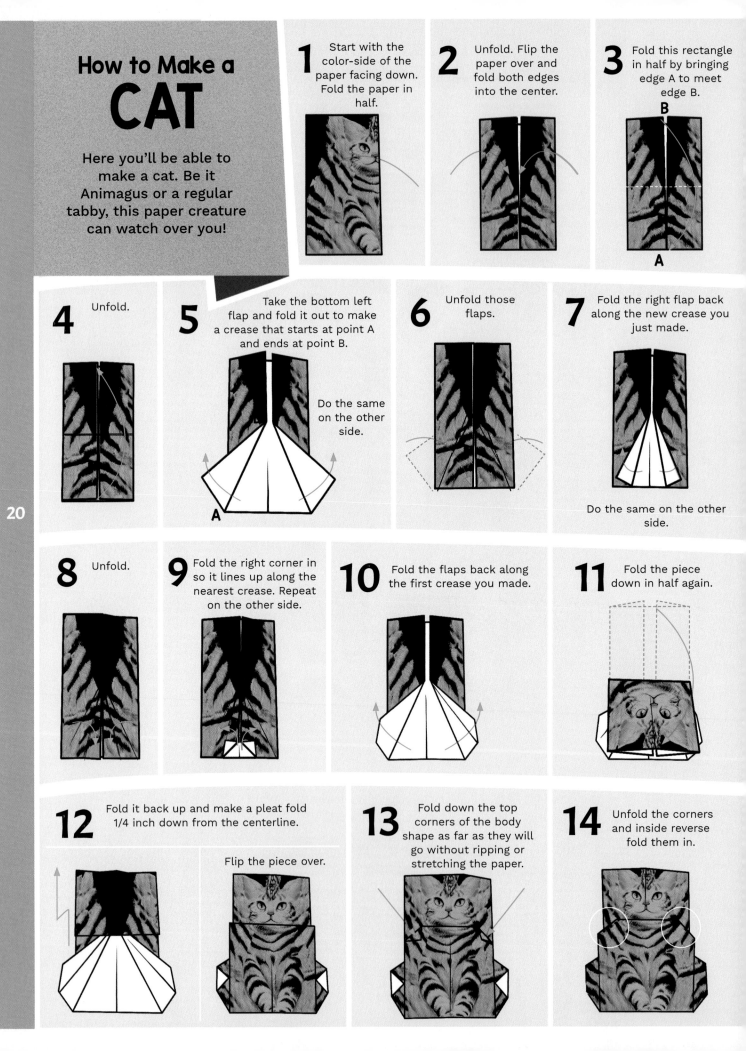

15 Flip the piece over.

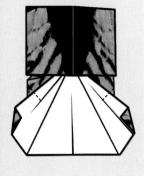

16 Fold up the bottom corners of the head as far as they will go without ripping.

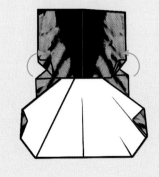

17 Take the top right corner and fold it down to meet the centerline. Do the same on the other side.

18 Fold the right flap back about 1/8 inch from the edge to form a cat ear. Do the same on the other side.

TIP: You might want to peek on the other side of your paper and make sure you're happy with the angle of your cat's ears.

19 Flip the piece over. Fold down the point of the head to flatten it out.

20 Pleat fold the sides of your cat and shape its paws how you'd like.

DONE!

OWL

Among the list of permitted animal companions at Hogwarts is an **OWL**. Owls are favored by many students because they can deliver mail. Harry's own bird, a beautiful snowy owl named Hedwig, was gifted to him by Hagrid in *Harry Potter and the Sorcerer's Stone*. Hedwig proved fiercely loyal to Harry during his years at Hogwarts; she also offered him comfort during his summers at the Dursleys'.

DIFFICULTY: ⚡ ⚡ ⚡ ⚡

How to Make an OWL

Create your own origami owl by following these steps, then complete the bonus step at the end to make another!

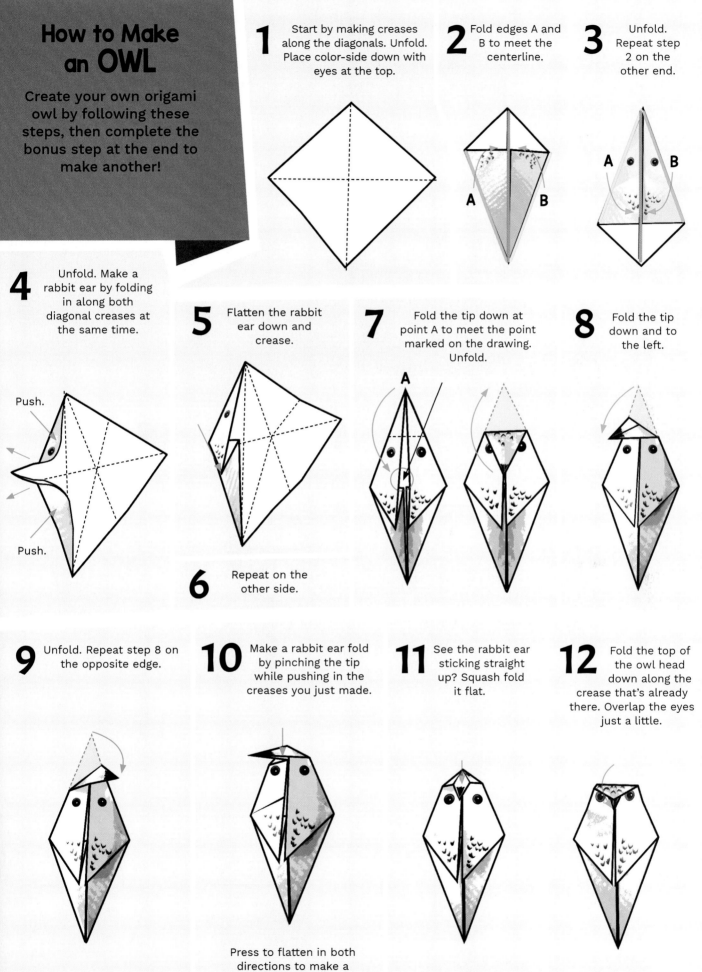

1 Start by making creases along the diagonals. Unfold. Place color-side down with eyes at the top.

2 Fold edges A and B to meet the centerline.

3 Unfold. Repeat step 2 on the other end.

4 Unfold. Make a rabbit ear by folding in along both diagonal creases at the same time.

Push.

Push.

5 Flatten the rabbit ear down and crease.

6 Repeat on the other side.

7 Fold the tip down at point A to meet the point marked on the drawing. Unfold.

8 Fold the tip down and to the left.

9 Unfold. Repeat step 8 on the opposite edge.

10 Make a rabbit ear fold by pinching the tip while pushing in the creases you just made.

Press to flatten in both directions to make a strong crease.

11 See the rabbit ear sticking straight up? Squash fold it flat.

12 Fold the top of the owl head down along the crease that's already there. Overlap the eyes just a little.

23

13 Lift up these two flaps. Flatten.

14 Fold the tip of each flap down to touch the side edge.

15 Fold down the head section. You want to make a crease that runs along the tops of the folds you just made.

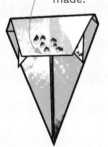

16 Fold back up. Make a pleat fold along this point.

17 Fold these tips up as far as they will go without ripping. Unfold.

18 Now make inside reverse folds at those corners. To do this, lift up each corner and push in.

19 Flip the owl over.

20 Fold the bottom point to the tip-top.

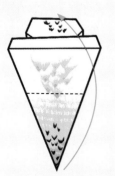

21 Fold edge A down to meet edge B.

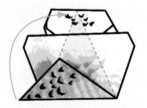

A

B

22 Unfold. Repeat step 21 on the other side.

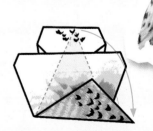

23 Unfold. Do a rabbit ear by pushing in on the creases you just made.

Make sure to push in both sides at the same time. Press to flatten.

24 Fold in the left edge of the owl's body.

25 Fold in the right edge.

26 Do your best to fold down the shoulder point to meet the horizontal crease.

27 Fold the sides of the head in on an angle.

28 Now we're going to make a little stand with the tail.

Fold in the tip.

29 Using the centerline as a starting point, fold up point A to meet point B.

A

30 Repeat on the other side. Then pull the tail out to make a stand.

31 Flip the owl over and stand it up. Curl in the tip of the wings.

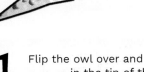

DONE!

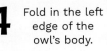

BONUS!
Make a **GREAT HORNED OWL** out of the brown textured paper in the back of this book!

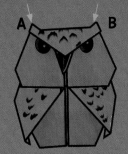

A   B

Pinch the corners of points A and B to make the "horns."

THE GOLDEN SNITCH

TWO PARTS

In Quidditch, there are four balls—the Quaffle, which scores points; the Bludgers, which attempt to distract players; and the **SNITCH**, a small golden ball with wings. The Snitch is nearly impossible to see and worth 150 points. A game of Quidditch is only complete when a team's Seeker catches it . . . or spits it out of their mouth and into their hand.

DIFFICULTY: ⚡ ⚡ ⚡ ⚡ ⚡

How to Make a GOLDEN SNITCH

The Snitch is made in two parts—the body and the wings. We'll begin with the body. The Snitch's body is made from what's known in origami as a water balloon base.

PART I
Body

1 To start your water balloon base, cut out the gold square with adult supervision and place color-side down.

2 Fold the paper in half both ways. Then unfold in half and fold diagonally both ways. Unfold. Your folds should look like this.

3 Place the paper color-side up. Fold in half.

4 With the open side down, inside reverse fold right side.

5 Repeat on the left side.

6 Bring the top layer of corners A and B to C. Press to crease.

7 Flip the piece over. Repeat step 6 to form a diamond.

8 Fold the top layer of points A and B in to the centerline.

Repeat on the back.

9 See how those triangles have made pocket flaps? Tuck corner A into pocket B and C.

10 Flip the piece over and repeat step 9 on the other side.

11 Flaps should be snug in their pockets.

TIP: Tape the flaps in to make your piece sturdier.

12 Rotate the piece. This end should have a hole in it.

13 Blow into this hole to inflate the balloon. You might need to gently open your folds first. Now the body is **COMPLETE!**

TIP: Blow from a small distance—don't press your lips directly to the paper. You don't want to cut your lip!

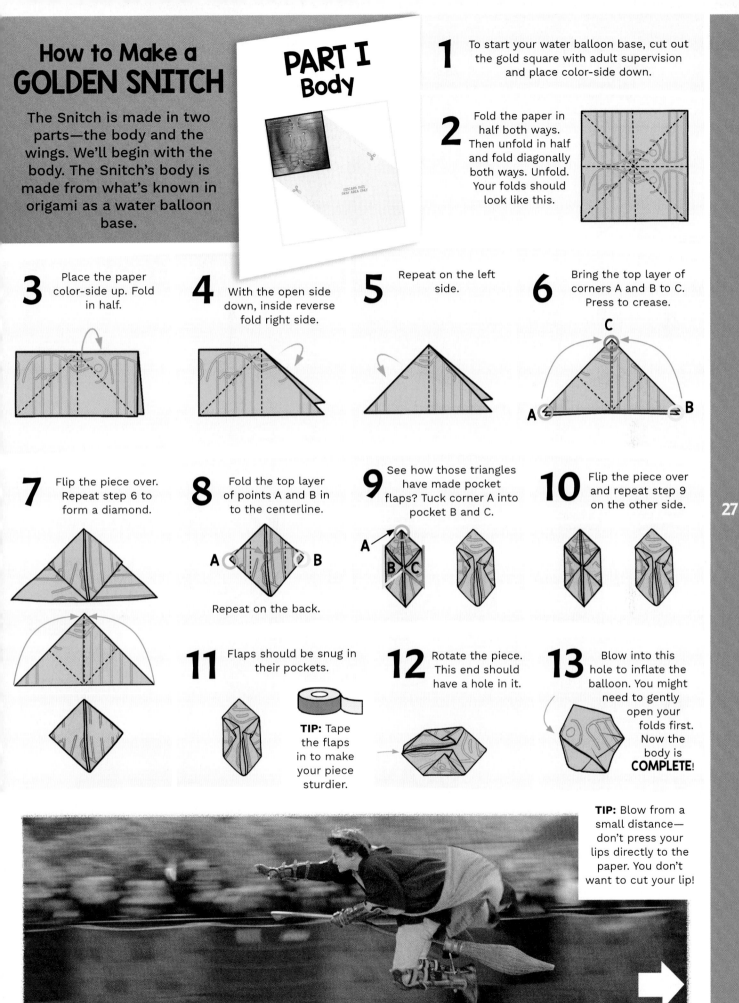

27

PART II
Wings

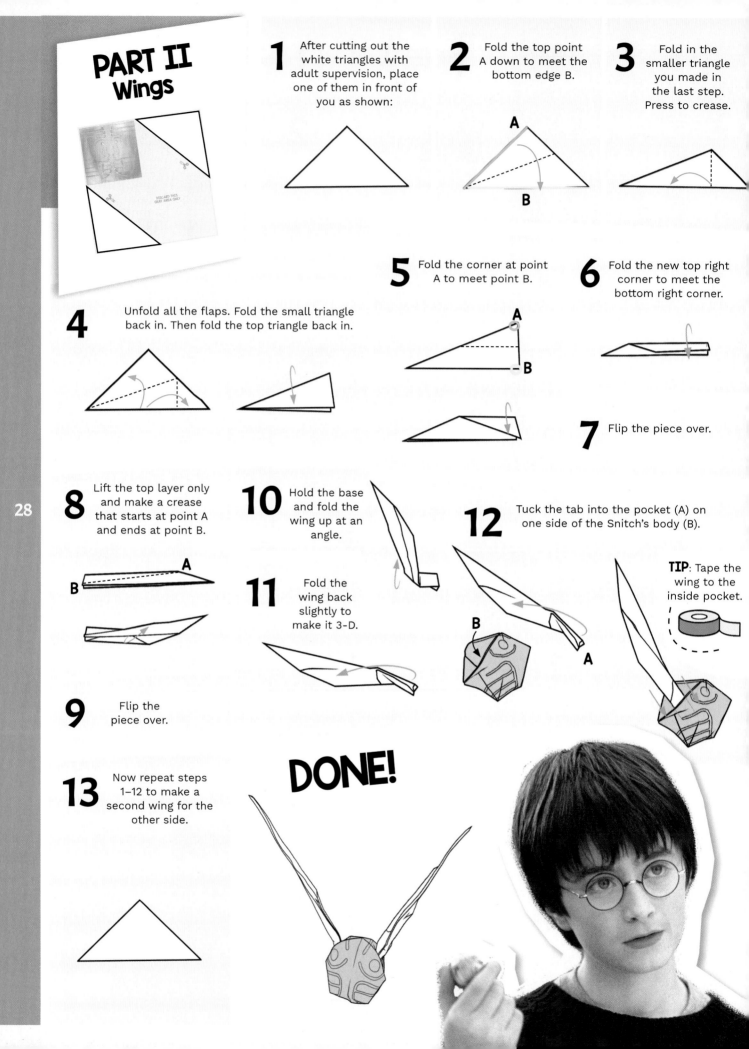

1 After cutting out the white triangles with adult supervision, place one of them in front of you as shown:

2 Fold the top point A down to meet the bottom edge B.

3 Fold in the smaller triangle you made in the last step. Press to crease.

4 Unfold all the flaps. Fold the small triangle back in. Then fold the top triangle back in.

5 Fold the corner at point A to meet point B.

6 Fold the new top right corner to meet the bottom right corner.

7 Flip the piece over.

8 Lift the top layer only and make a crease that starts at point A and ends at point B.

9 Flip the piece over.

10 Hold the base and fold the wing up at an angle.

11 Fold the wing back slightly to make it 3-D.

12 Tuck the tab into the pocket (A) on one side of the Snitch's body (B).

TIP: Tape the wing to the inside pocket.

13 Now repeat steps 1–12 to make a second wing for the other side.

DONE!

DRAGON

DRAGONS are impressive magical creatures that can breathe fire. In *Harry Potter and the Sorcerer's Stone*, Hagrid told Harry that he always wanted a dragon. Hagrid's wish came true when he met a stranger with a dragon egg in his pocket . . . but because it's illegal to own a dragon, Hagrid's prized Norwegian Ridgeback was sent to live with Ron's brother Charlie Weasley in a dragon sanctuary in Romania.

DIFFICULTY:

How to Make a DRAGON

For this piece, you can make a Norwegian Ridgeback, Chinese Fireball, Ukrainian Ironbelly—or all three! We recommend beginning with the Norwegian Ridgeback. To create creases, you may want to use an optional Popsicle stick. You'll also need scissors for this piece with adult supervision.

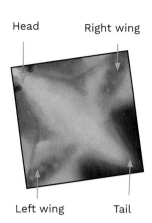

Head

Right wing

Left wing

Tail

1 Start by folding a bird base. Look back at the introduction on page 9 for step-by-step instructions.

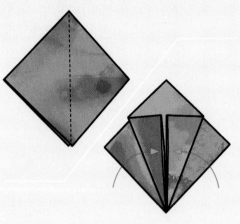

2 Place the square base so it looks like a diamond. The two flaps that move like legs should be at the bottom.

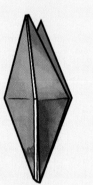

3 Take the top layer of that right "leg" and fold it to meet the centerline. Do the same thing on the left side.

4 Flip the whole piece over and repeat step 3 on the other side.

5 Now it's time to start making the head. With your scissors, make two small cuts toward the bottom of the right "leg." If you look inside, you'll see three layers. Do not cut the center layer.

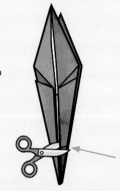

6 Fold out the flaps you just made. This is the head.

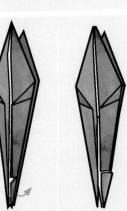

7 Rotate the piece so it looks like this.

8 Take the opposite "leg"—the one without the head—and pull it across the body on a diagonal as far as it will go without tearing.

Press hard to make a crease. This will become the tail.

9 Fold the tail back horizontally to make a new crease. Unfold.

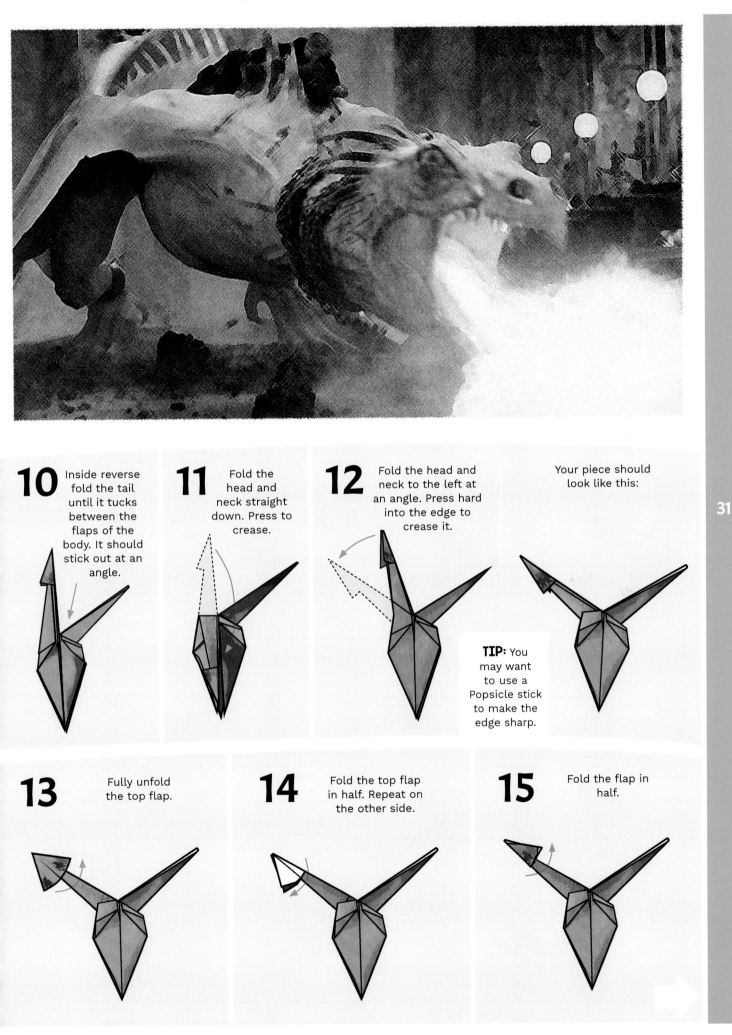

10 Inside reverse fold the tail until it tucks between the flaps of the body. It should stick out at an angle.

11 Fold the head and neck straight down. Press to crease.

12 Fold the head and neck to the left at an angle. Press hard into the edge to crease it.

Your piece should look like this:

TIP: You may want to use a Popsicle stick to make the edge sharp.

13 Fully unfold the top flap.

14 Fold the top flap in half. Repeat on the other side.

15 Fold the flap in half.

16 Now we're going to fold the wings. Lift the top layer of the wing flap and fold it up as far as it will go. Repeat on the other side.

It should look like this:

17 Fold the top of the wing down and out so it lines up to crease A. Press hard to crease.

A

18 Fold edge A so it lines up with edge B.

A **B**

19 Unfold the wing a little bit. Now flatten it out. Bring point A to point B.

A **B**

20 Unfold the wing.

21 Pleat fold your dragon's wings to shape them how you'd like.

22 Repeat steps 19-21 on the other side.

23 Crimp down the head so it's facing forward.

24 Tuck in the point of the nose to make the head a little smaller.

25 Curl the tail so the dragon stands up.

DONE!

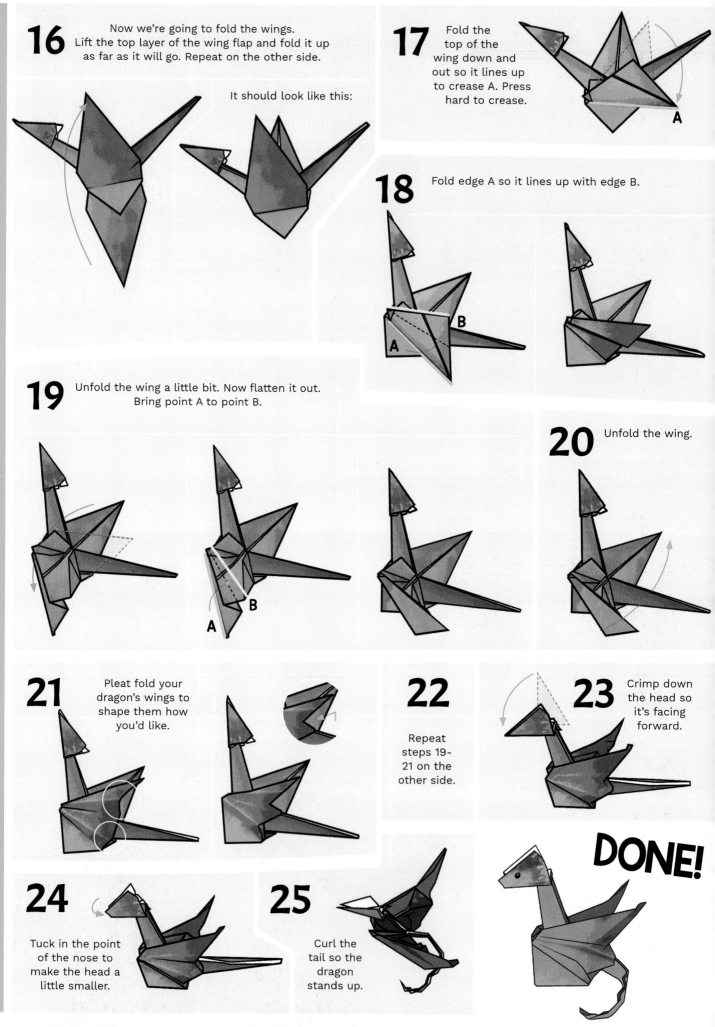

FIREBOLT BROOMSTICK

ONE PART

The **FIREBOLT** is an elite, fast, and elegant model of broomstick. After Harry's Nimbus 2000 was destroyed by the Whomping Willow in *Harry Potter and the Prisoner of Azkaban*, his godfather, Sirius Black, anonymously sent him the Firebolt via owl post. Harry is seen using his Firebolt during the first task of the Triwizard Tournament as well as while captaining the Gryffindor Quidditch team in *Harry Potter and the Half-Blood Prince*.

DIFFICULTY: ⚡ ⚡ ⚡ ⚡ ⚡

How to Make a
FIREBOLT BROOMSTICK

Begin by making a kite base. You can find base step-by-step instructions on page 8. Make sure to fold your broomstick in half along the handle, then fold in.

1 Unfold the kite base. Rotate your paper 180 degrees, then fold into a new kite base using the same centerline crease.

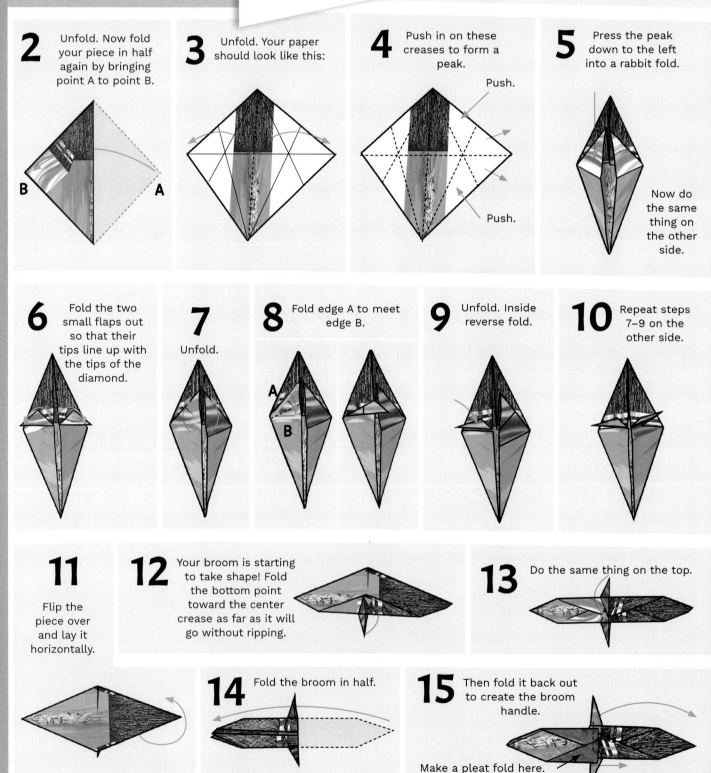

2 Unfold. Now fold your piece in half again by bringing point A to point B.

3 Unfold. Your paper should look like this:

4 Push in on these creases to form a peak.

Push.

Push.

5 Press the peak down to the left into a rabbit fold.

Now do the same thing on the other side.

6 Fold the two small flaps out so that their tips line up with the tips of the diamond.

7 Unfold.

8 Fold edge A to meet edge B.

9 Unfold. Inside reverse fold.

10 Repeat steps 7–9 on the other side.

11 Flip the piece over and lay it horizontally.

12 Your broom is starting to take shape! Fold the bottom point toward the center crease as far as it will go without ripping.

13 Do the same thing on the top.

14 Fold the broom in half.

15 Then fold it back out to create the broom handle.

Make a pleat fold here.

16 Now it's time to shape the handle and make it thin. Take the top edge of the handle and fold it to meet the centerline. Squash fold to press it down.

17 Repeat on the other side.

18 Flip the broom over.

19 Fold the bristles toward the handle.

20 Fold the bristles back and make a pleat fold.

New crease.

21 Fold the point of the bristles under and tuck them in.

22 Inside reverse fold the two stirrups at these outer points.

23 Fold the whole broom in half lengthwise to give a 3-D shape. Press hard.

24 Pleat fold the broom handle to make it look like a lightning bolt.

DONE!

CHOCOLATE FROG
and Box

THREE PARTS

CHOCOLATE FROGS are edible sweets—but if not eaten fast enough, they can jump up and hop away! Harry learns this on his very first Hogwarts Express trip, when he and Ron bond over a set of Chocolate Frogs from the Trolley Witch. Later, in *Harry Potter and the Prisoner of Azkaban*, Harry learns that Chocolate Frogs can soothe some of the rather unpleasant aftereffects from Dementors. The Chocolate Frogs also come packaged with a card of a famous witch or wizard, such as Albus Dumbledore.

DIFFICULTY:

To make the Chocolate Frog, start with the paper color-side down in front of you. We'll begin by making lots of creases. When you're done, you'll be able to make your frog hop by pressing on its rear with your finger and letting go!

PART I
Chocolate Frog

1 Fold the paper in half.

2 Fold the top right edge from point A to point B. Then unfold and repeat on the left side.

A
B

3 Repeat step 2 on the bottom.

4 Slide your middle fingers under line A and pinch in, folding the top of the origami piece in as a triangle. Press to crease.

A

TIP: If you're having difficulty at this step, sharpen the crease at point A with your fingers to help you.

5 Repeat step 4 on the bottom. Now you should have a smaller diamond!

A

6 Fold only the front layer of points A and B to point C.

C
B   A

7 Fold these two flaps out.

A

8 Repeat steps 6 and 7 at the bottom.

9 Flip the piece over. Then fold the bottom corner up as shown.

10 Fold the left and right sides in to the centerline of the triangle you just made. Press to crease.

11 Mountain fold the bottom of the piece as pictured.

12 Valley fold the frog's legs underneath.

TIP: Tape your Chocolate Frog's front legs underneath its head to keep your piece sturdy.

Now your frog is **COMPLETE!** Time to make the box on the next page.

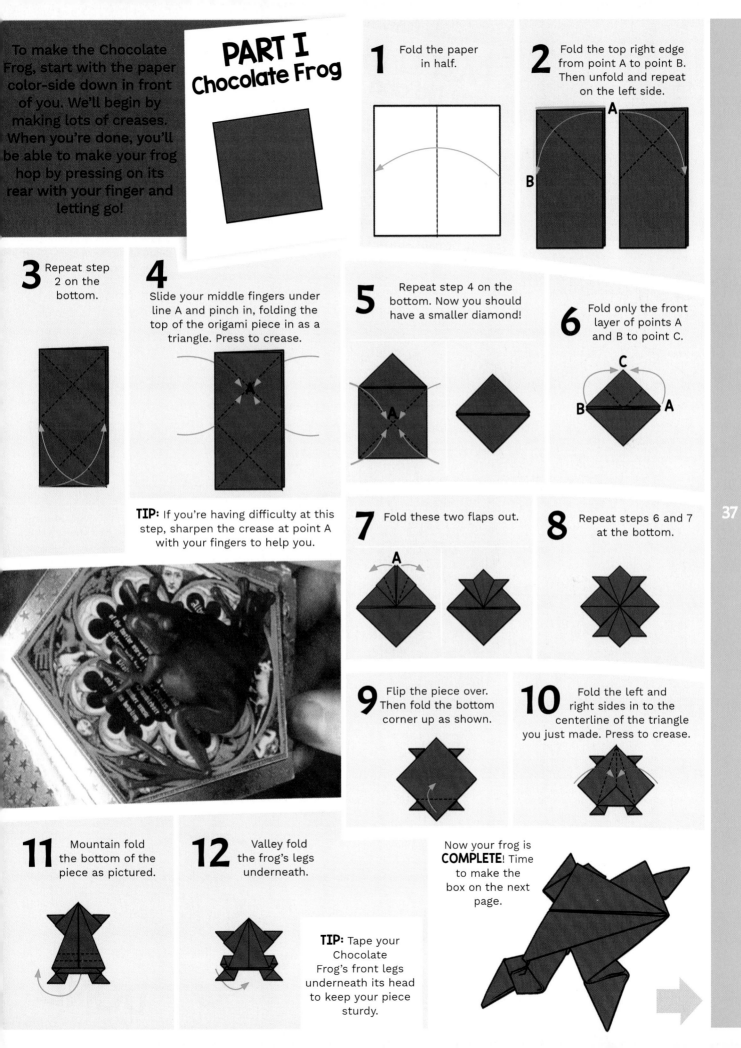

Take the printed paper and cut around the outside edges to make a pentagon. Always make sure to have adult supervision when handling scissors. The time you spend making folds and creases for this piece will pay off when you shape your box later on.

PART II AND III
Box Lid and Base

1 Fold the paper in half. Unfold.

2 Fold the paper in half again along each axis.

TIP: There are five of these lines on a pentagram. Start at one corner and fold all five.

3 When you're done, your creases should look like this:

4 Bring the bottom edge of the pentagon up to meet the center point.

Press to crease. Unfold.

5 Fold the bottom edge up to meet the new crease you just made. Unfold.

A

6 Repeat steps 4–5 along all four remaining outer edges. When you're done, the creases on your paper will look like this:

7 Fold the bottom edge and the left edge up along the inner creases to make a rabbit fold.

8 Fold the rabbit ear over so its top lines up with the edge of the box. Make a crease.

9 Repeat steps 7–8 on all the corners.

10 Fold the lip of the box down along the highest crease, one side at a time.

Be careful to tuck in any flaps.

11 Repeat this process using the larger pentagon for the top of the frog box. Then put your box pieces together with your frog inside.

TIP: Tape your rabbit folds in to keep them sturdy.

DONE!

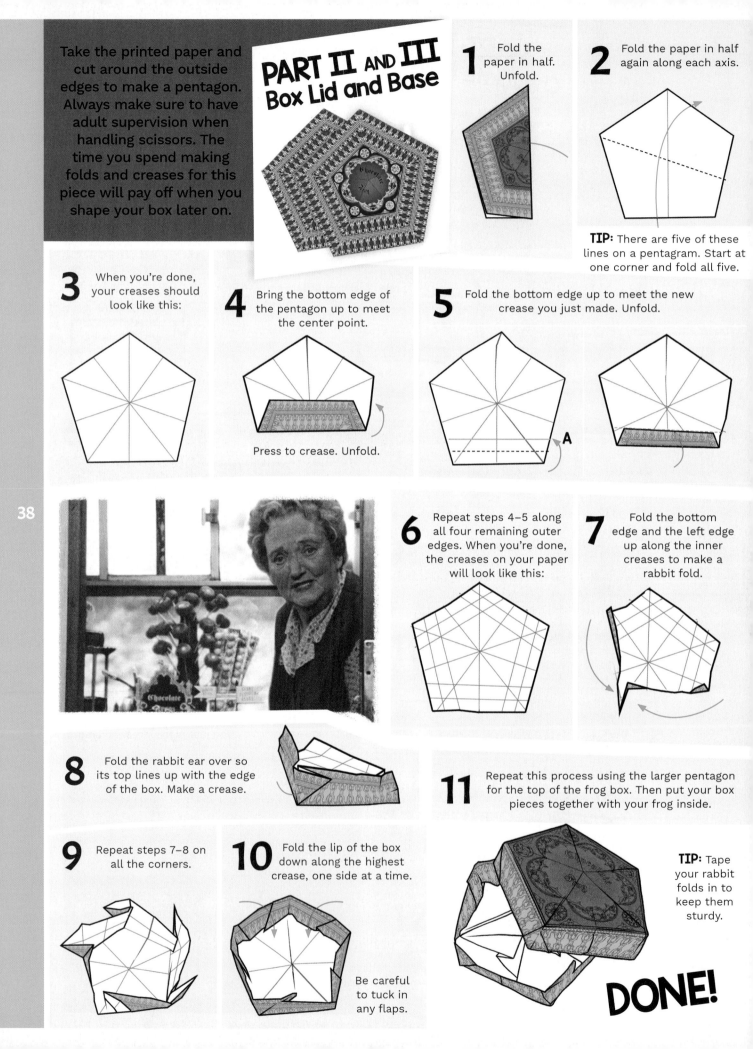

38

UNICORN

UNICORNS are magical creatures that resemble horses and have horns on their heads. If unicorn blood is consumed, the drinker can be kept alive (even if they are in the most dire of peril), but their life becomes reduced to a half, cursed life. Unicorn hair is often used to make wands; some known wielders of unicorn-hair wands included Ron Weasley, Draco Malfoy, and Cedric Diggory.

DIFFICULTY: ⚡ ⚡ ⚡ ⚡ ⚡

How to Make a UNICORN

You will need scissors to make this unicorn—be sure to have adult supervision! Start with a square base. Look back at the introduction on page 8 for step-by-step instructions.

1 Hold the square base so it looks like a diamond. The layers that open should be at the bottom.

2 Continue as if you were going to make a bird base. Fold the sides of the top layer in toward the center.

3 Flip the diamond over. Fold in the sides again.

4 Fold down the top triangle.

5 Unfold the flaps. Your piece should look like this:

6 With your scissors, cut along the centerline stopping at the base of the upside-down triangle. Make sure to cut through all the layers of paper.

Stop here.

7 Fold only the top layer of each bottom triangle as far as it will go without ripping the paper.

8 See the new diamonds you've created? Fold them in half lengthwise.

9 Flip the piece over and unfold the flaps. Repeat steps 7–8 on the other side.

10 Rotate the piece as shown. Fold up the bottom triangle.

11 Take the top left flap and inside reverse fold it so that it lines up with the bottom left flap. On the top right flap, fold the tip under as shown to create a neck.

12 Unfold the right side. Open up the head by unfolding the back layer, too. Take your scissors and cut along the centerline of the head flap. Repeat on the other layer.

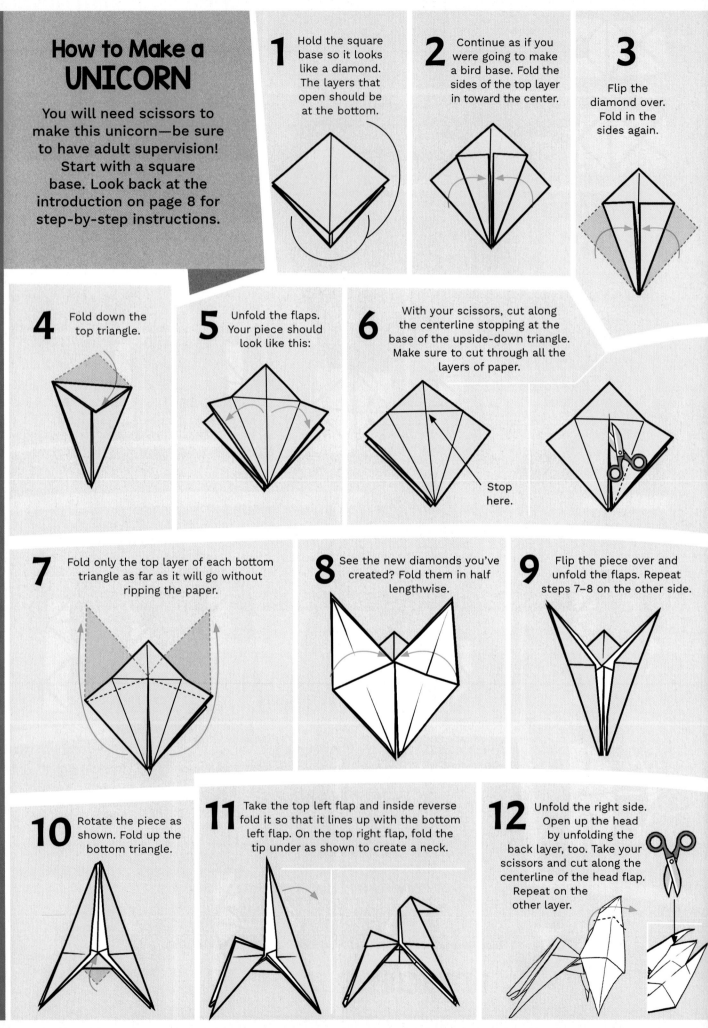

13 Fold everything back up.

14 Now for the horn. Reach in the middle of your unicorn's head and pull the middle two flaps up.

15 When you close the head back up, you'll see a unicorn horn!

TIP: Cut or fold the second "horn" into the head to make your origami piece nice and clean.

16 Inside reverse fold the nose so it's not as pointy.

17 For the tail, reach inside the rear legs and pull out the center layer.

Inside reverse fold this layer until it sticks up and out.

18 Shape the front leg by folding it under and back.

Press to crease.

19 Pleat fold the bottom of the front leg down.

20 Make a pleat in the back leg to give it dimension. Repeat step 20 on the hind leg.

21 Repeat steps 18-20 on the other side for the other legs.

22 Inside reverse fold the bottom tip of the leg to flatten out the hooves.

23 Open up the tail a little bit and make two pleat folds to give it dimension. The tail should look like a lightning bolt!

TOP VIEW

Close the tail back up.

TIP: Push down the folds above the tail to add more shape.

BONUS: Draw in your unicorn's eyes!

DONE!

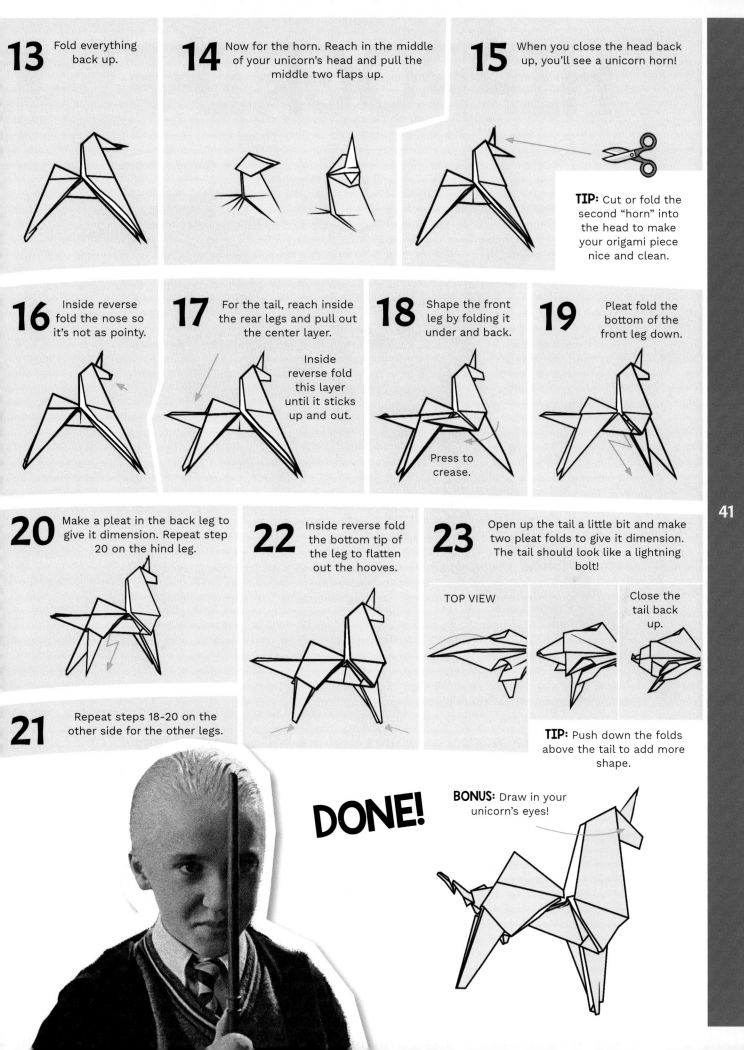

HIPPOGRIFF

HIPPOGRIFFS are magical creatures that are half eagle, half horse. Their bodies, back legs, and tails resemble horses', but their heads and front legs are those of an eagle. Hagrid introduced third-year students to a Hippogriff named Buckbeak in *Harry Potter and the Prisoner of Azkaban*. However, Draco Malfoy provoked Buckbeak into attacking him. This caused Buckbeak to be sentenced to death by the Ministry . . . but thankfully, Harry and Hermione rescued him with a Time-Turner, and Buckbeak was able to escape with Sirius Black.

DIFFICULTY: ⚡ ⚡ ⚡ ⚡ ⚡

How to Make a HIPPOGRIFF

Be proud like a Hippogriff when you finish this piece! You may want to use an optional Popsicle stick to press down on your creases.

1 Start by folding a bird base. Ensure the head texture is on the outside.

2 Flip up the top layer.

3 Fold the whole bird base in half lengthwise. Press hard to crease.

The head section (with dark feathers) should be as shown.

4 Outside reverse fold the outer layer of the bottom point.

5 Inside reverse the top fold.

6 Lift up the wing. Pull out the paper that's underneath it and flatten it upward. Repeat on the other side.

7 Rotate your piece so the neck is pointing up. Crimp the point outside the neck to create the head.

8 Outside reverse fold the point of the beak.

9 Do another inside reverse fold to finish the Hippogriff's beak. Now you finished the head!

10 Next, fold the top wing down. Repeat on the other side.

11 Make three crimp folds in the wing. Press down hard on the creases.

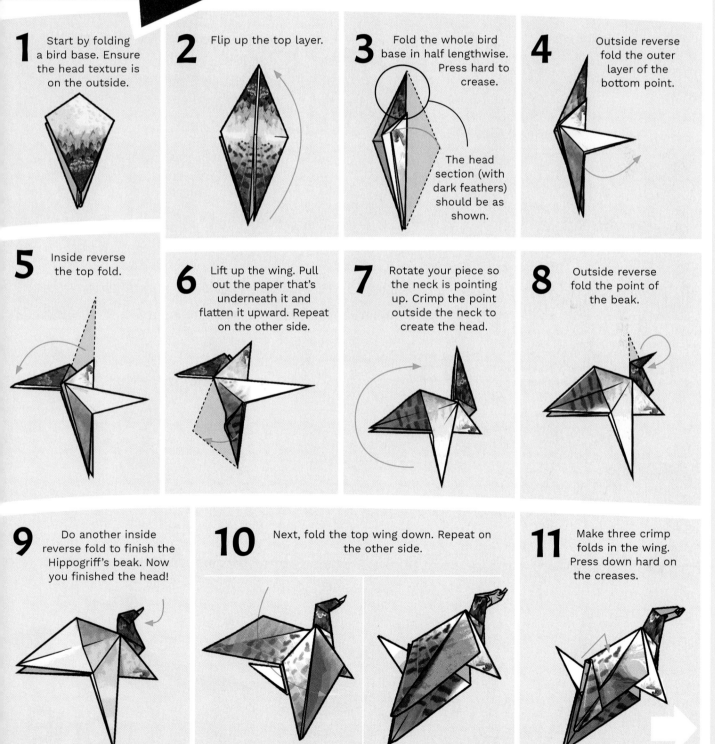

12 Tug the wing out a little to give it some dimension.

13 Repeat steps 10–12 on the other wing.

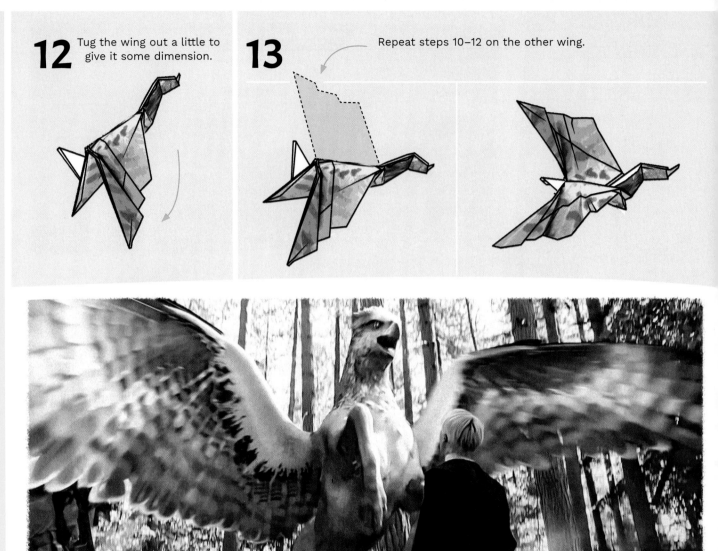

14 Squash the triangle at the Hippogriff's chest to flatten it out. Press to crease.

Squash here.

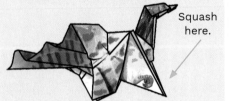

15 Inside reverse fold the tail so it sticks up at an angle.

Squash the tip of the tail to create a diamond head.

16 Push in the middle crease to make two little feet.

BOTTOM VIEW

Once your Hippogriff is folded, draw in the eyes.

FAWKES the PHOENIX

ONE PART

As Professor Dumbledore explained in *Harry Potter and the Chamber of Secrets*, **PHOENIXES** are birds with incredible healing abilities. They are loyal creatures, immune to Basilisks, and possess impressive strength. When it is time for a phoenix to die, it does so, but is then reborn from the ashes. Phoenix feathers also make for good wand cores. Harry Potter and Lord Voldemort's wands had "twin cores," meaning their feathers came from the same phoenix. Coincidentally, that phoenix was Dumbledore's own Fawkes.

DIFFICULTY: ⚡ ⚡ ⚡ ⚡ ⚡

How to Make FAWKES the PHOENIX

We're going to use a variation of a bird base to make this fiery phoenix. You will also need a pair of scissors—be sure to use them with adult supervision!

1 Start with the paper color-side down.

2 Fold the paper in half. Unfold.

3 Fold it in half the other way. Unfold.

4 Fold the paper diagonally. Unfold.

5 Bring the bottom edge to the centerline. Press to crease.

6 Repeat step 5 on the left edge of the paper. Unfold.

Your paper should look like this:

7 Pinch in the lower left corner. Use the creases you made in steps 5–6 to make a rabbit ear.

8 Flatten out the corner.

9 Fold down the rabbit ear.

10 Now pull it up and squash fold.

11 Fold the piece in half to form a triangle. Press to flatten.

12 Fold it in half again to form a smaller triangle.

13 Stick your finger inside one of the flaps and make a squash fold.

14 Flip the piece over. Fold the point up to make a crease.

Squash fold.

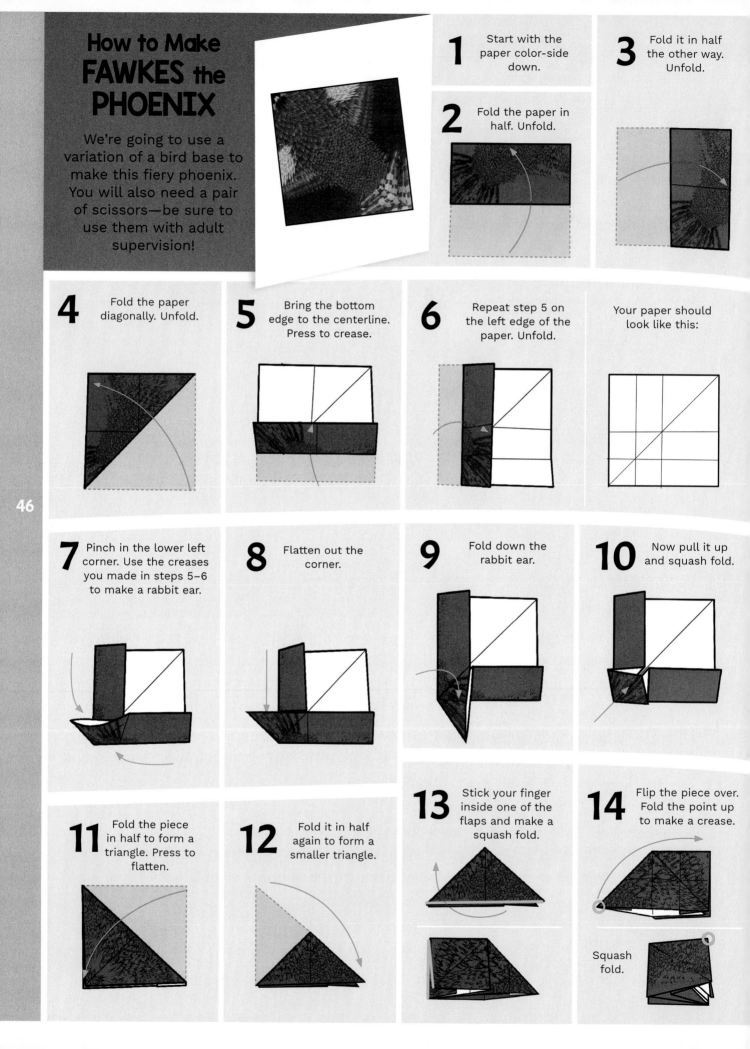

15 Look familiar? You've made a square base!

16 Take the lower right-hand edge and fold it in to the centerline.

17 Unfold. Petal fold. There are extra layers of paper inside. Do your best to keep them in place.

18 Flip the piece over. Repeat steps 16–17 on the other side.

19 Notice that there are two pointed flaps at the bottom. One has more paper inside than the other. Fold the thinner flap in to meet the center.

20 Repeat step 19 on the other side.

21 With your own scissors, make a small cut near the bottom of the thinner flap. Cut only the top layer. Repeat on the other side.

Cut here.

22 Now that you have the cuts, open up those flaps to make a head.

23 Fold open the top layer of the left side.

24 Fold the head section up.

25 Fold the right half of that head section over to the left.

26 Now look inside the bottom flap of your piece. Grab the middle layer of paper and pull it out.

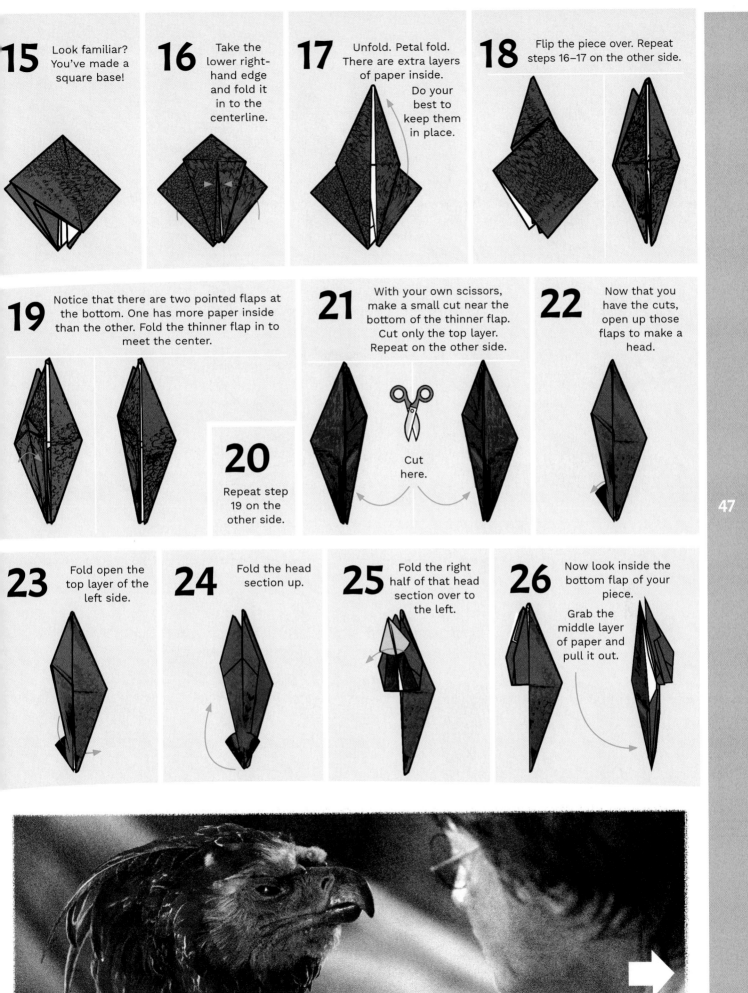

27 Make a cut along the center crease.

28 Fold open the two sides.

29 Fold edge A to meet edge B.

A

B

Repeat on the other side.

30 Fold the new edge A to meet edge B.

A

B

31 Repeat steps 29–30 on the other side.

32 Fold the wing flaps back on both sides.

33 Flip the wings up toward the head.

Pull out the tail feathers.

34 Fold along the existing creases like an accordion. You may have to reverse the direction of some of the creases.

35 Repeat steps 33–34 on the other side.

36 Flip down the wing flaps.

37 Taking the head in one hand and the tail in the other, crimp the tail up in between the folds of the body. Press to crease.

38 Open the body section. Fold one edge down into the center. Do the same thing on the other side.

TAIL: CLOSE UP

39 Close it back up. Bend the head down and forward.

Crimp the sides of the head out and over the neck.

40 Reverse fold in and out to form the beak.

41 Fan out the tail feathers.

DONE!

48

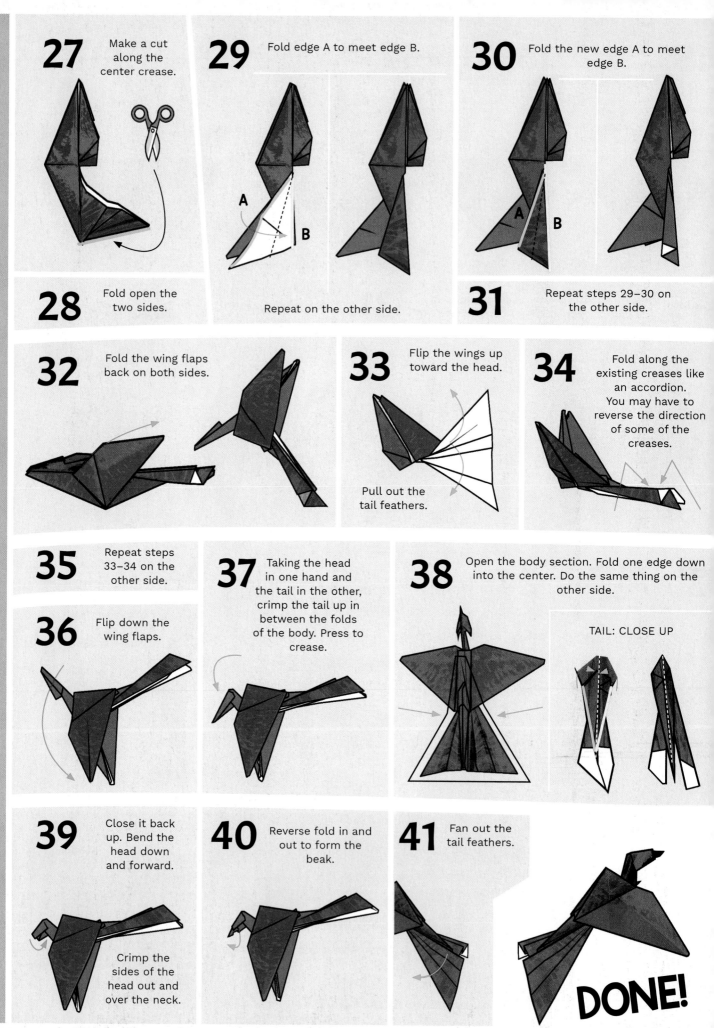

FLUFFY

TWO PARTS

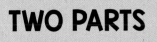

FLUFFY is a three-headed dog that guarded the Sorcerer's Stone. Although Fluffy was vicious, he could be lulled to sleep with a bit of music. Hagrid accidentally revealed this information to the stranger who gifted him a dragon egg—and the stranger (later revealed to be Professor Quirrell) used this intel to enchant a harp and keep Fluffy at bay.

DIFFICULTY: ⚡ ⚡ ⚡ ⚡ ⚡

How to Make FLUFFY

You will need two pieces of paper to make this dog. You will be assembling Fluffy after he's been lulled to sleep. You will need tape, scissors, a pen, and adult supervision for this piece.

PART I Heads

1 Fold into a bird base. Lift up the bottom flap to create a diamond.

Each half of the diamond has two flaps at the bottom.

2 Fold the left flap over.

Your piece should look like this:

3 Flip the diamond up.

Fold the left flap over to the right.

4 Flip the piece over again. See the two triangles sticking up?

Push up the diamond one final time.

5 Fold the whole piece in half as shown.

6 You should have three separate flaps for the heads at the top.

Inside reverse fold the top flap. Press to crease.

7 Open up that new fold a little bit and fold point A down into point B.

B

A

8 Make a crease.

9 Make a pleat fold.

10 Fold in point A to meet crease B.

A
B

11 Press the head flat. You've now made the first head!

50

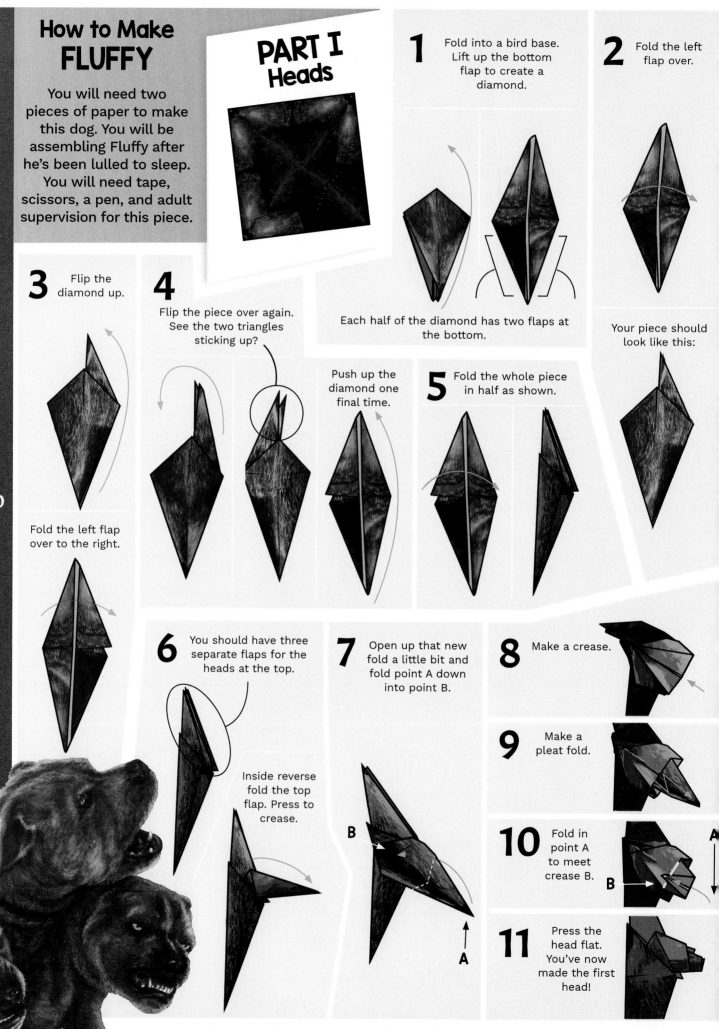

12 Repeat steps 8–11 on the remaining two flaps.

13 Take the point of the triangle that is sticking up and inside reverse fold into the center of the center head.

14 Fan out the heads. Squash fold both triangular flaps between each head.

Fold all heads back together.

15 Take the bottom of the neck and fold it back horizontally. Press hard to crease.

16 Unfold. Fold in edge A to line up with edge B. Repeat on other side.

B   A

17 Inside reverse fold the bottom section. Press it flat.

18 With your scissors and adult supervision, cut the top layers of the white lines to shape Fluffy's ears. Now your heads are **COMPLETE**!

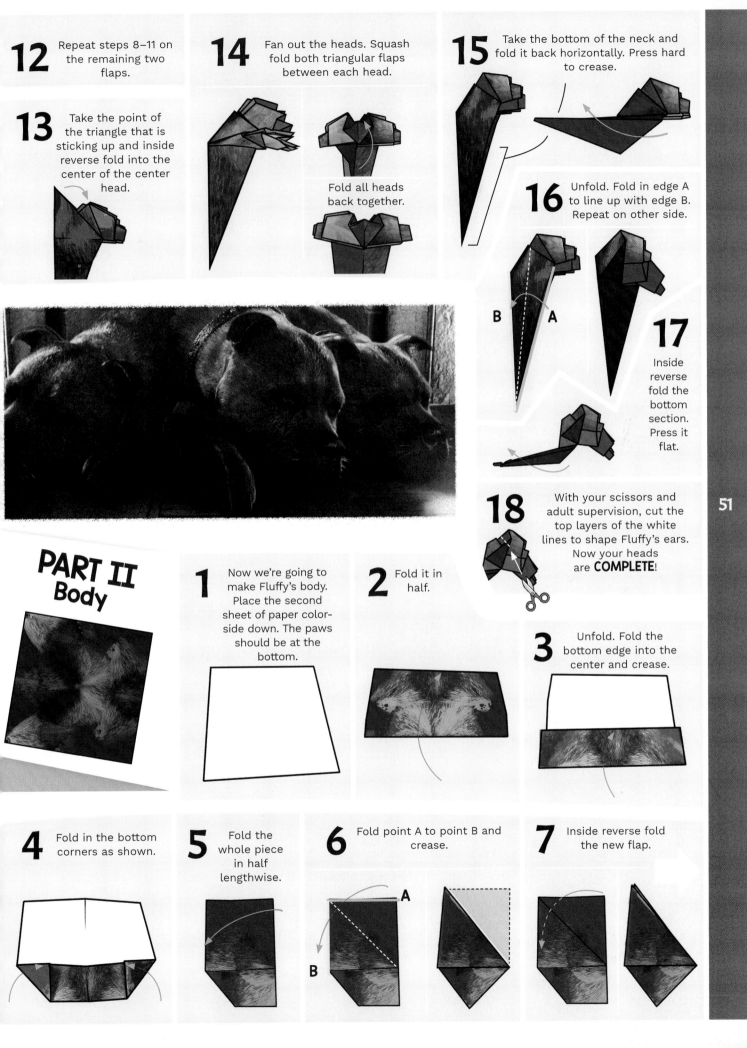

PART II
Body

1 Now we're going to make Fluffy's body. Place the second sheet of paper color-side down. The paws should be at the bottom.

2 Fold it in half.

3 Unfold. Fold the bottom edge into the center and crease.

4 Fold in the bottom corners as shown.

5 Fold the whole piece in half lengthwise.

6 Fold point A to point B and crease.

A

B

7 Inside reverse fold the new flap.

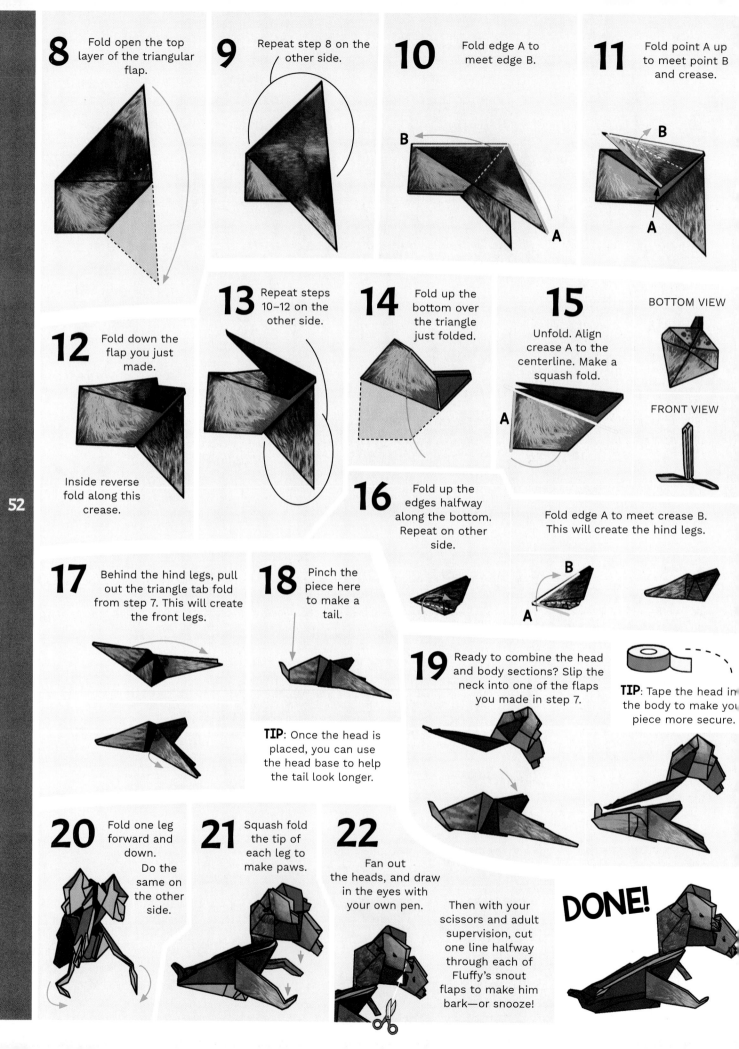

8 Fold open the top layer of the triangular flap.

9 Repeat step 8 on the other side.

10 Fold edge A to meet edge B.

11 Fold point A up to meet point B and crease.

12 Fold down the flap you just made.

Inside reverse fold along this crease.

13 Repeat steps 10–12 on the other side.

14 Fold up the bottom over the triangle just folded.

15 Unfold. Align crease A to the centerline. Make a squash fold.

BOTTOM VIEW

FRONT VIEW

16 Fold up the edges halfway along the bottom. Repeat on other side.

Fold edge A to meet crease B. This will create the hind legs.

17 Behind the hind legs, pull out the triangle tab fold from step 7. This will create the front legs.

18 Pinch the piece here to make a tail.

TIP: Once the head is placed, you can use the head base to help the tail look longer.

19 Ready to combine the head and body sections? Slip the neck into one of the flaps you made in step 7.

TIP: Tape the head in the body to make you piece more secure.

20 Fold one leg forward and down.
Do the same on the other side.

21 Squash fold the tip of each leg to make paws.

22 Fan out the heads, and draw in the eyes with your own pen.

Then with your scissors and adult supervision, cut one line halfway through each of Fluffy's snout flaps to make him bark—or snooze!

DONE!

STAG PATRONUS

In *Harry Potter and the Prisoner of Azkaban*, Harry learned how to cast the Patronus Charm, which, when performed correctly, creates a corporeal shape known as a **PATRONUS**. Each individual's Patronus is unique to them. While Ron's Patronus is a Jack Russell terrier and Hermione's is an otter, Harry's takes the form of a stag, which he later learned was the unofficial, unregistered form of his father's Animagus. Harry's **STAG PATRONUS** protected him on numerous occasions, including from the Dementor's Kiss in *Harry Potter and the Prisoner of Azkaban*.

DIFFICULTY: ⚡ ⚡ ⚡ ⚡ ⚡

How to Make a STAG PATRONUS

No need to incant *Expecto Patronum* to form this Patronus! However, you will need scissors and tape for this guardian.

1 Start with the paper color-side down.

2 Fold in half.

3 With adult supervision, cut along the crease you just made. You should have two strips.

4 Fold one strip in half. Unfold.

5 With adult supervision, cut along the crease. Throw away one half. Then tape the other half to edge A of your long strip. This should create a paper that is 50 percent longer than it was.

6 Now you have one extra-long strip.

7 Fold the paper in half lengthwise. Unfold.

8 Fold the taped-in square in half as shown. This will form a triangle.

9 Unfold. Fold the taped-in square in half diagonally the other way.

10 Flip the paper over. Fold the left edge in to line up with the crease at point A. Unfold. Your piece should look like this:

A

11 Flip the paper over. Make a squash fold.

12 Lift one layer of this flap.

13 Squash the flap flat. Press to flatten.

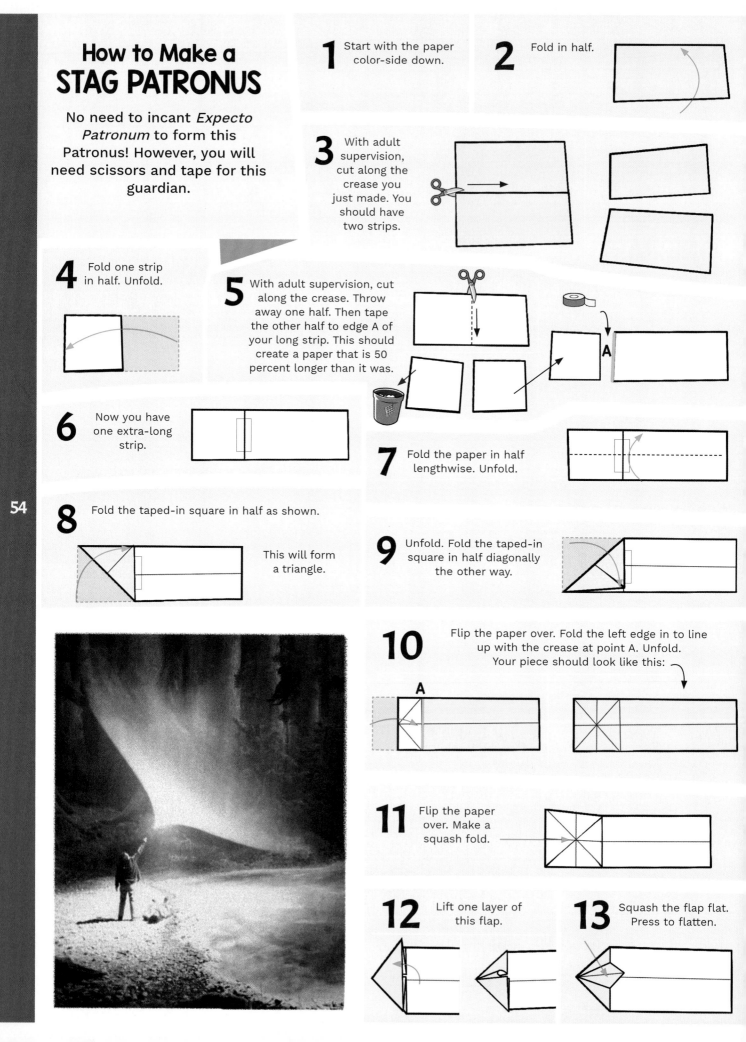

14 Prepare for a petal fold by making new creases.

Fold edge A and B to meet the centerline.

B

A

Unfold.

15 Stick your finger inside the petal fold. Lift the bottom point A up to meet point B. Massage carefully along the creases you made in step 14.

16 Flip down the petal fold.

17 Close the diamond.

18 Repeat steps 15–17 with the other flap.

19

Flip to the center flap.

20 Flip the piece over.

21 Fold edge A and B to the centerline. Press to crease. Unfold.

A

B

22 Take edge A and fold it down to meet crease B.

B

A

23 Repeat step 22 on the other side.

A

B

24 Push on the creases you just made at the same time until the triangular piece at the top moves forward and in.

25 Fold the entire top section back and under along the horizontal crease that is taped.

26 Take the bottom corner of the large rectangle and fold it up along the horizontal edge. Press to crease at the arrow. Repeat on the other side.

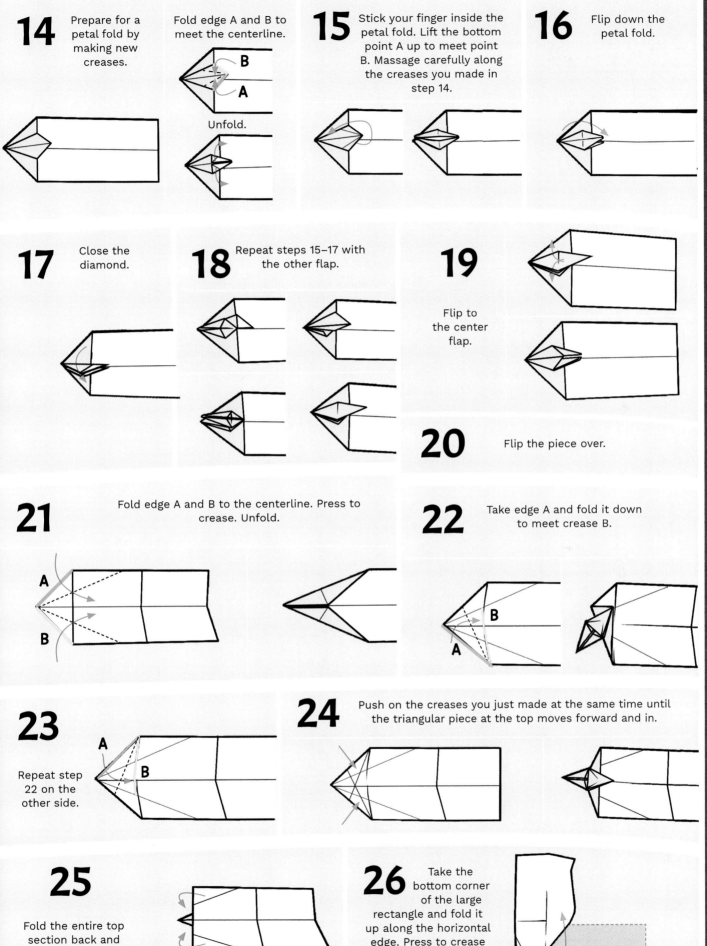
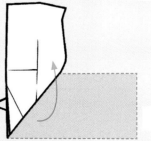

27 Unfold. Fold in half lengthwise. Fold up corner to meet edge A. Repeat on the other side.

A

Your piece should look like this:

28 Unfold. Take edge and fold down the nose to touch the center point marked here.

29 Fold the head section back along the bottom edge.

30 Flip the piece over. Fold edge A to touch the center point marked here.

A

31 Fold in the same edge one more time.

32 Flip the stag over.

33 Fold both sides in to the centerline.

34 There are pockets at all four corners of the stag.

One at a time, slide your finger up into each pocket to open it up. Then squash fold it flat.

35 Pleat fold it back.

36 Fold point A to meet edge B. Repeat on the other side.

B
A

37 Open flap A.

38 Fold in these corners. Press to crease.

39 Fold flap back in as shown.

40 Flip the piece over. Fold the entire piece in half.

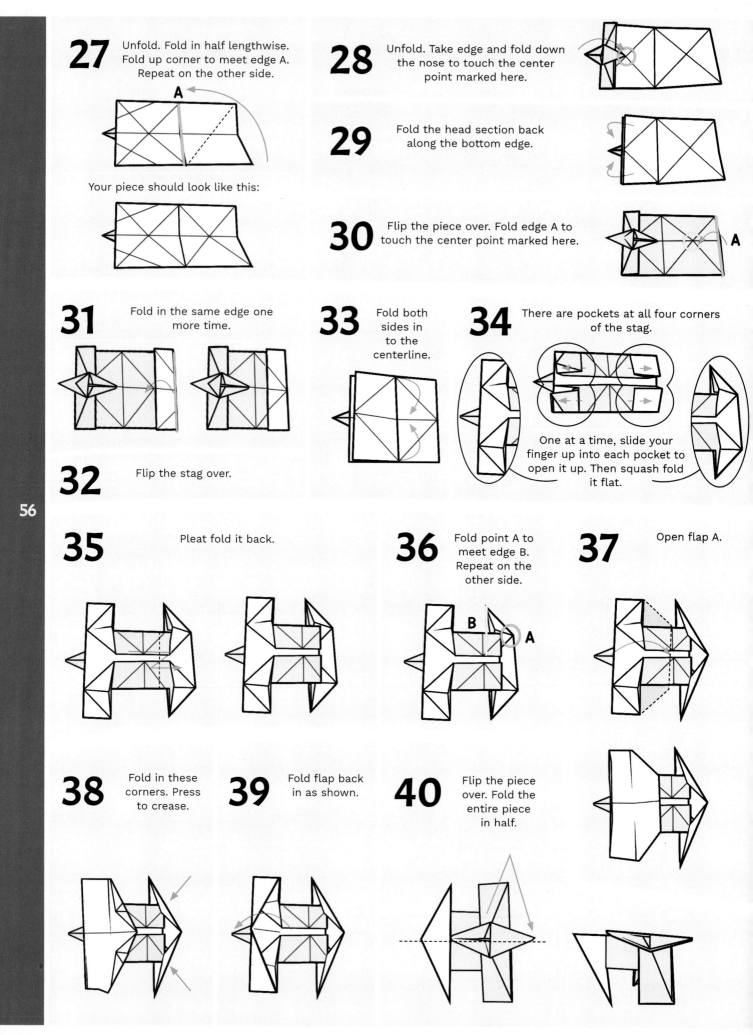

41 On the opposite end, grab the back of the head and swivel it up until the front legs come to a point. Press to hold the crease in place.

Grab here.

42 Make a tail by doing an inside reverse fold on the bottom tip. Then another inside reverse fold.

43 Press to hold the crease in place by folding in edge A to wrap around the leg.

44 Open up the head flap.

45 With adult supervision, cut along the center crease. Do the same thing on the other side.

46 Close the head back up.

47 To shape the legs, pinch each hind leg and bend it back slightly. Pinch each front leg and bend it forward slightly.

48 Inside reverse fold the tip of the nose.

49 Use your fingers to shape your stag's antlers however you'd like!

50 Inside each antler is another flap. Pull each out and bend them back to give the antlers dimension.

Curl the front flaps forward to shape your stag's ears.

DONE!

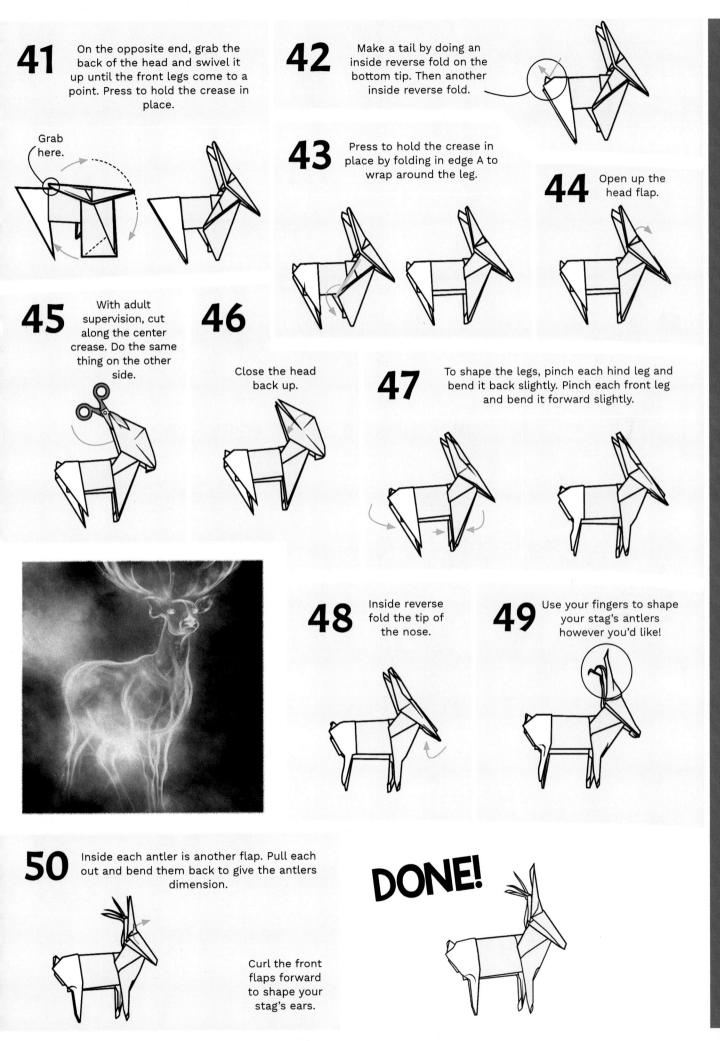

HOGWARTS

THREE PARTS

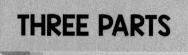

Founded at the turn of the last millennium, **HOGWARTS SCHOOL OF WITCHCRAFT AND WIZARDRY** is considered by many (mainly British) wizards to be the best wizarding school in the world. First-year students are sorted into one of four houses—Gryffindor, Hufflepuff, Ravenclaw, and Slytherin—by the Sorting Hat in the Great Hall. The castle and grounds are expansive, though many key scenes in the Harry Potter films take place in the Great Hall and the Great Tower.

DIFFICULTY: ⚡⚡⚡⚡⚡

How to Make
HOGWARTS

Hogwarts will be made in three parts. We'll start with the back side of the Great Hall, and we'll prepare our paper by making a bunch of creases to help the castle take shape.

1 Place the paper with Hogwarts on top white-side up. Fold it in half.

2 Unfold. Fold the bottom up to the centerline but only crease half an inch on the left edge.

Crease here.

3 Unfold. Fold the bottom up so edge A meets crease B.

B
A

4 Unfold. Fold edge A to meet crease B. Press to crease all the way across.

A
B

Your paper should look like this:

Crease only the edge.

5 Unfold. Fold the paper in half like you did in step 1.

Fold the paper in half along the existing crease.

6 Fold the bottom edge A up to edge B. Press to re-make the crease. Unfold.

B
A

7 Fold in half the other way.

8 Unfold. Fold both edges to the centerline.

9 Unfold the right flap. Fold edge A to edge B.

B
A

10 Unfold. Fold edge A to edge B.

B
A

11 Unfold and repeat on the other side. Unfold again.

59

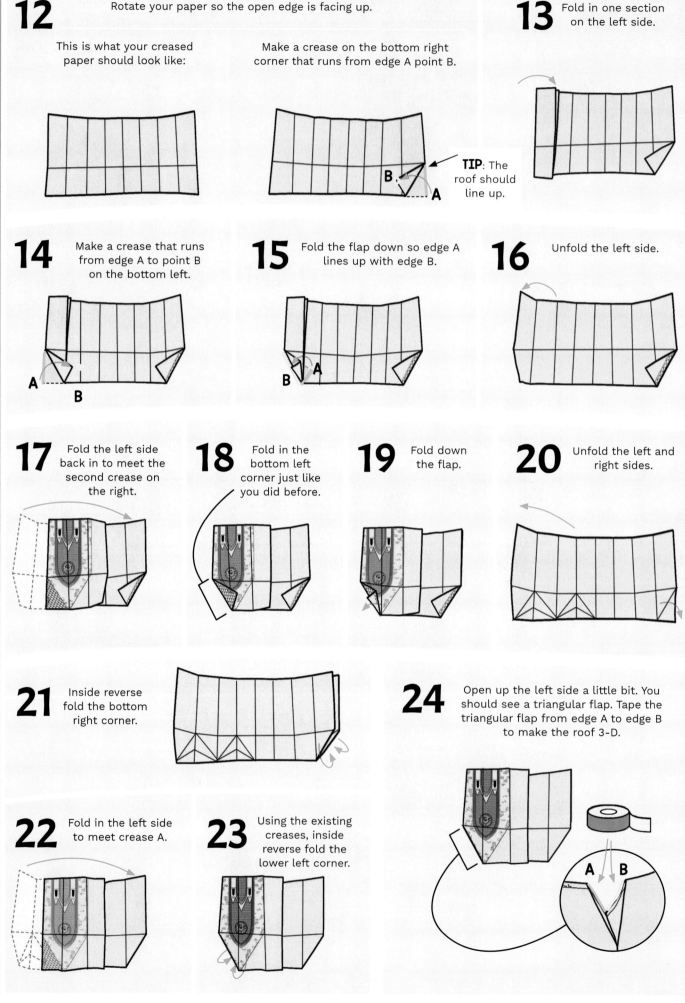

12 Rotate your paper so the open edge is facing up.

This is what your creased paper should look like:

Make a crease on the bottom right corner that runs from edge A point B.

TIP: The roof should line up.

B A

13 Fold in one section on the left side.

14 Make a crease that runs from edge A to point B on the bottom left.

A B

15 Fold the flap down so edge A lines up with edge B.

B A

16 Unfold the left side.

17 Fold the left side back in to meet the second crease on the right.

18 Fold in the bottom left corner just like you did before.

19 Fold down the flap.

20 Unfold the left and right sides.

21 Inside reverse fold the bottom right corner.

24 Open up the left side a little bit. You should see a triangular flap. Tape the triangular flap from edge A to edge B to make the roof 3-D.

A B

22 Fold in the left side to meet crease A.

23 Using the existing creases, inside reverse fold the lower left corner.

25

Re-crease line A to bend the roof.

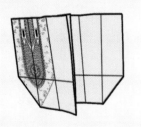

A

Tada! The back of the Great Hall is **COMPLETE**!

26

Repeat steps 24–25 along edges A and B.

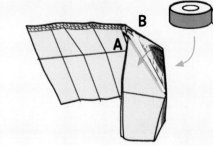

B

A

PART II
Great Hall: front

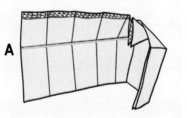

Now it's time to use what you've learned to fold the front of the Great Hall.

1

Start by repeating steps of the Great Hall. Stop right before the castle is about to become 3-D. Rotate the Great Hall 180 degrees so the open end faces down.

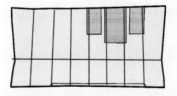

2 Now it's time to make the three turrets. With your scissors and adult supervision, cut along the top layer of the six highlighted vertical creases.

TIP: Cut off the two skinny strips if they're getting in the way.

3 Your paper should look like this:

4 Fold flap B up as far as it will go. Fold A and C flaps just slightly lower.

A B C

5 Make another crease at the base of each flap. This will help the tower stay upright.

6 Pinch the top of each flap in half to find the center point.

7 Unfold. At the top of each flap, make a crease that runs from point A to point B.

A
B

8 Repeat step 7 in the other direction.

62

9 Fold the tips in so they don't stick out.

10 Fold the peaks of the towers back so they are out of the way when you put the front and back of the Great Hall together.

11 Flip the piece over. Use the same series of inside reserve folds you used to make the back of the Great Hall 3-D.

12 Take a look at the back half of your Great Hall. It has a flap on the long end that will fit into the short end of the Great Hall front.

13 Connect the the Great Hall at both ends by sliding the flaps into one another. Tape these sections together.

TIP: To keep your origami sharp, tape the turrets up inside the origami!

14 On the inside of the Great Hall, fold in the bottom corner to lock the two halves. Push the towers back up on the front side.

The front is **COMPLETE!**

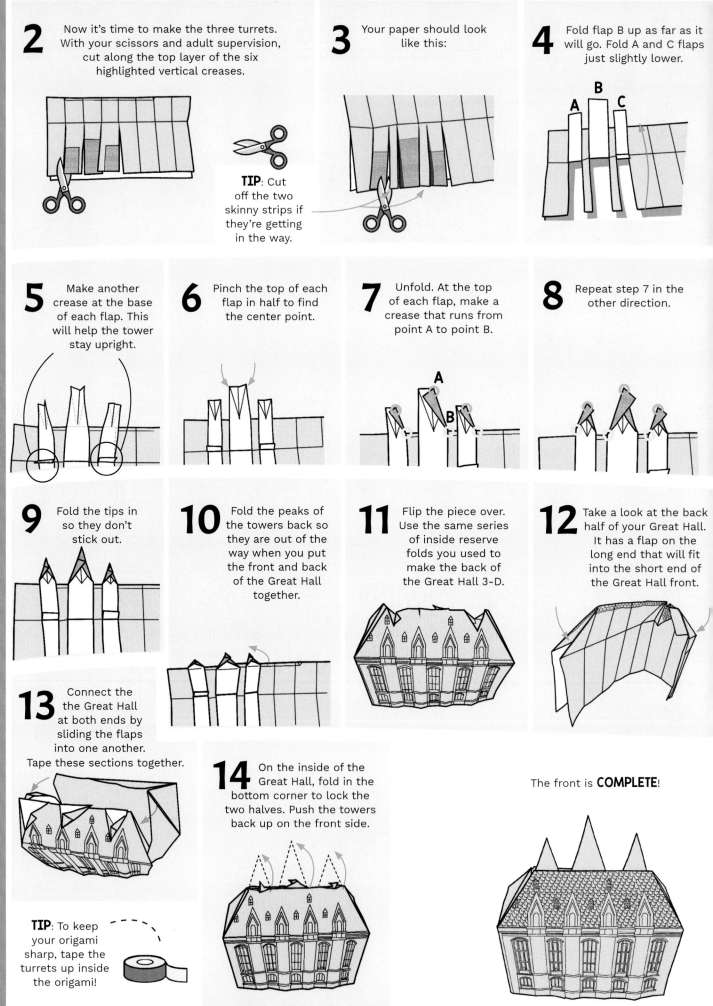

Time for Hogwarts's finishing touch—the tower!

PART III
The Great Tower

1 Place the paper white-side up. Using the three towers as a guide, fold it into thirds. Close the paper.

2 Fold the paper in half lengthwise but only crease the top third. This will be where the roof is. Unfold.

Crease here.

3 Open the left flap.

4 Fold down edge A to crease B.

B A

5 Fold down edge A to crease B as shown.

B A

Unfold.

6 Fold the left side in.

7 Repeat steps 4–6 on the left side.

8 Fold in edge A to crease B. Repeat on the other side.

A A

B B

9 Fold in edge A to crease B. Repeat on the other side.

10 Unfold. Your piece should look like this:

11 Fold the right flap in.

12 Inside reverse fold the top right corner along the existing creases.

Inside reverse fold here.

13 It's time to make the three towers that stick out. Do another inside reverse fold as shown.

14 With adult supervision, cut from the tip of the triangle you just made to the first crease. Your piece should look like this:

15 Fold the top two flaps you cut back inside. Now it's time to make the tower 3-D.

16 Look inside the tower. Fold the flap in toward the crease.

17 Using the edges of the paper as a guide, push in the tips of the tower and tuck the triangular flap inside.

18 Fold toward the inner crease to lock it in place.

19 Pinch the top of the tower together. Carefully tape edge A to edge B so that it is sturdy.

20 Stick your hand inside the tower and carefully push it out to give your piece shape. Stand the tower up next to the rest of the castle.

DONE!

SORTING HAT

CAULDRON

✂ ⟶

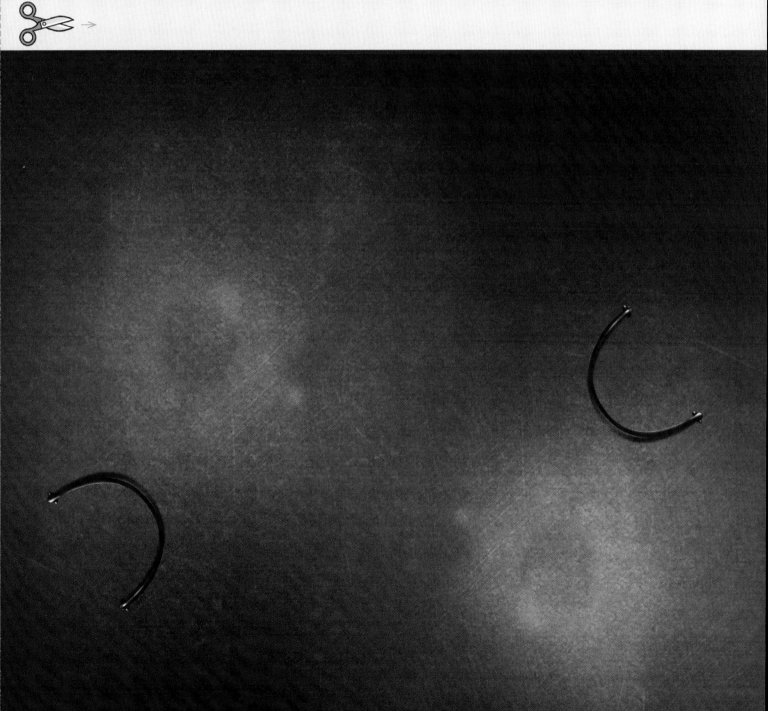

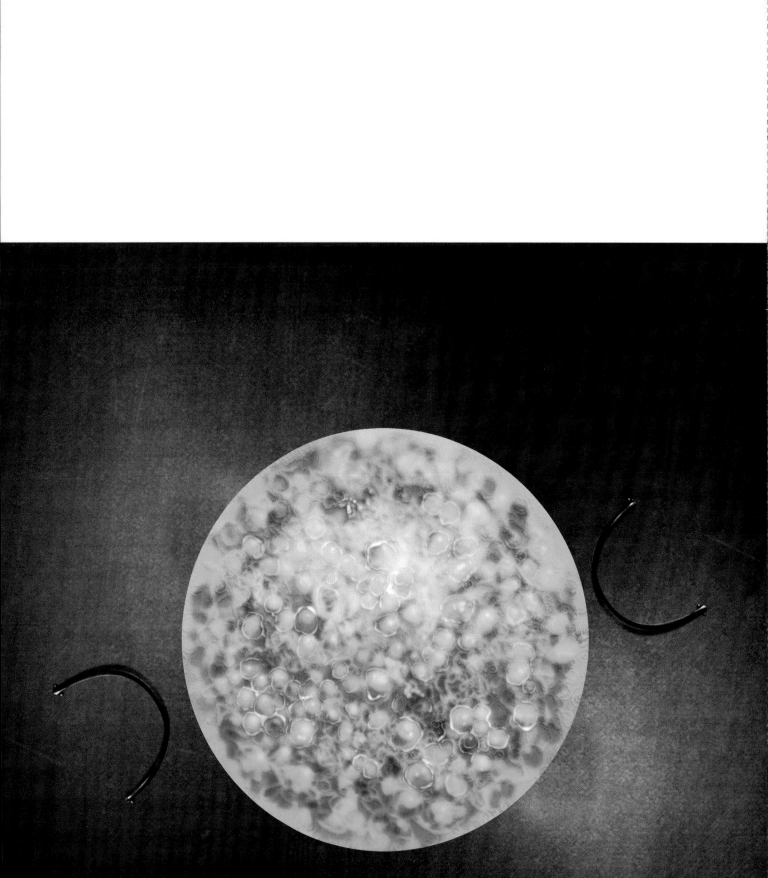

HOWLER

HOWLER

DIFFICULTY:

CAT

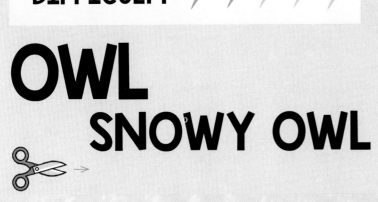

DIFFICULTY: ⚡ ⚡ ⚡ ⚡ ⚡

OWL
SNOWY OWL

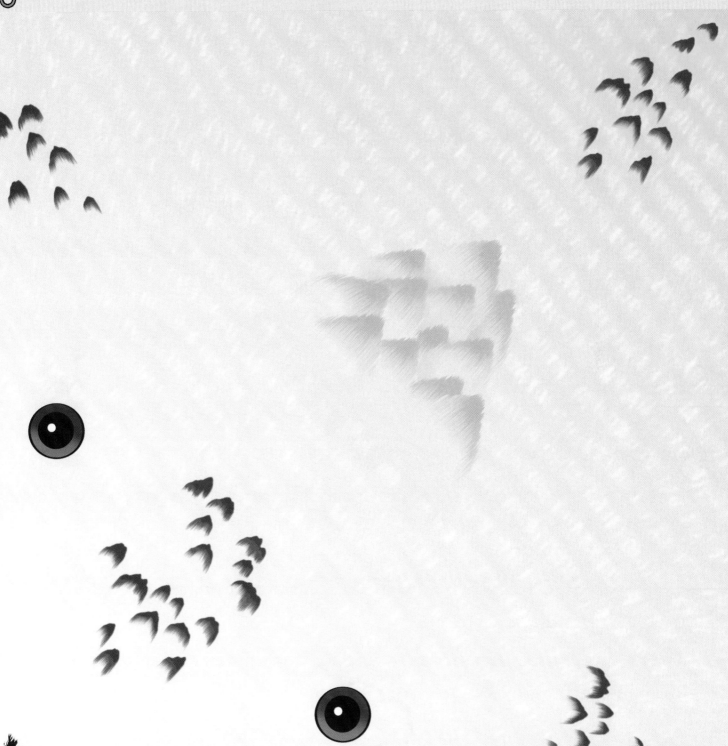

OWL
GREAT HORNED OWL

THE GOLDEN SNITCH

DISCARD THIS
GRAY AREA ONLY

DRAGON
NORWEGIAN RIDGEBACK

DRAGON
CHINESE FIREBALL

DRAGON
UKRAINIAN IRONBELLY

FIREBOLT BROOMSTICK

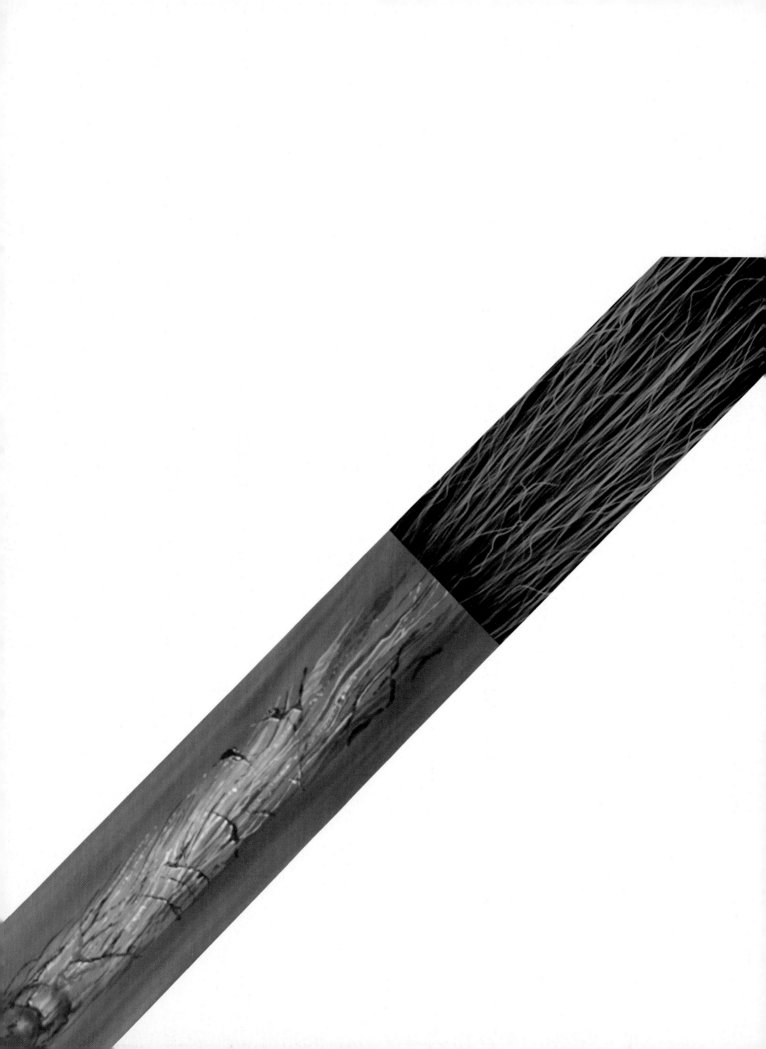

CHOCOLATE FROG
I. FROG

CHOCOLATE FROG
II. BOX (TOP)

CHOCOLATE FROG
III. BOX (BOTTOM)

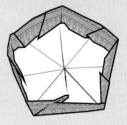

UNICORN

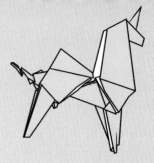

HIPPOGRIFF

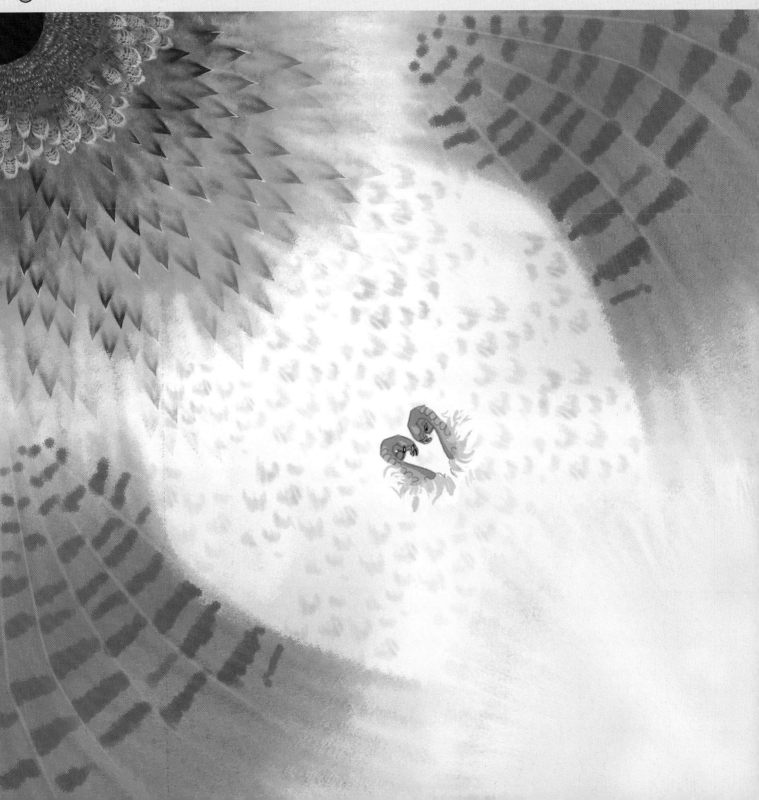

FAWKES THE PHOENIX

FLUFFY
I. HEADS

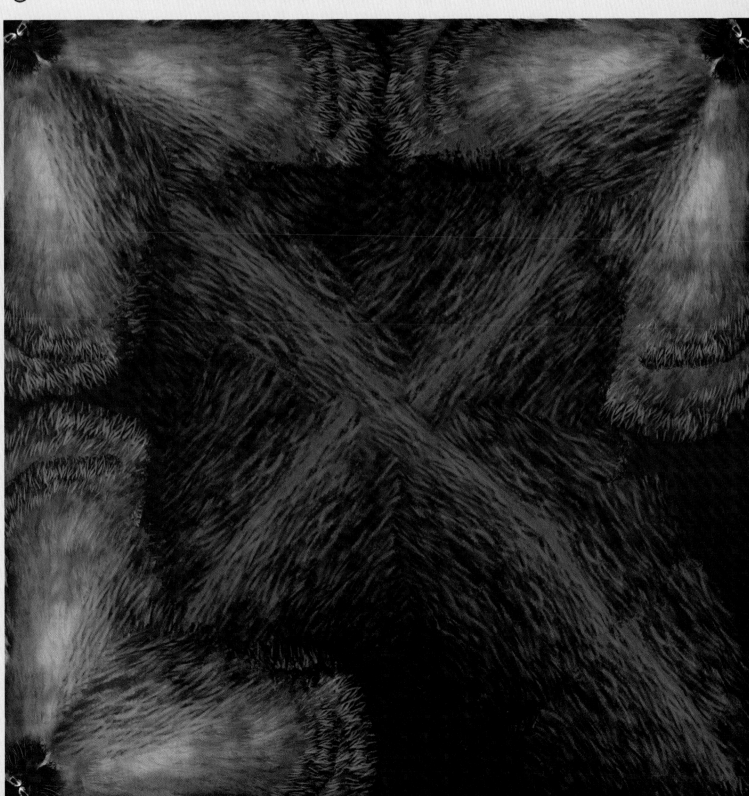

FLUFFY
II. BODY

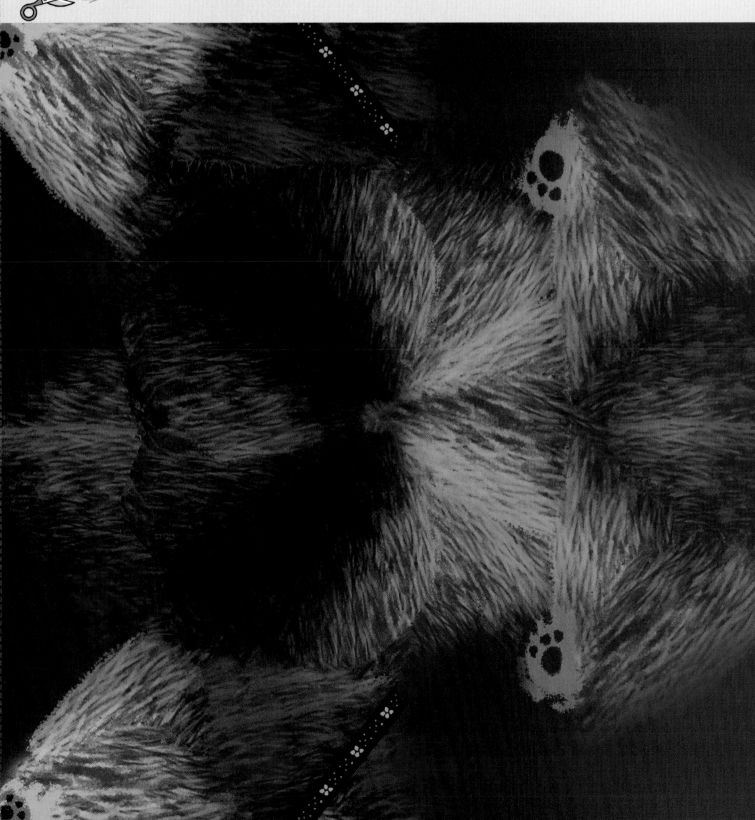

DIFFICULTY: ⚡⚡⚡⚡⚡

STAG PATRONUS

✂ ⇢

HOGWARTS
I. GREAT HALL: BACK

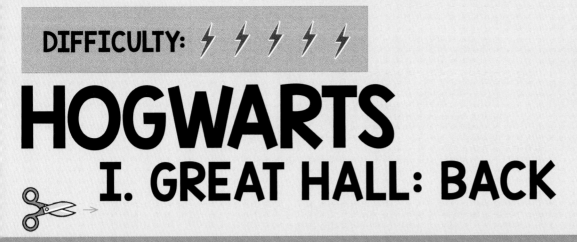